Abraham
the Friend of God

Abraham
the Friend of God

Hamilton Smith

GOSPEL FOLIO PRESS
P. O. Box 2041, Grand Rapids, MI 49501-2041
Available in the UK from
JOHN RITCHIE LTD., Kilmarnock, Scotland

Published by Gospel Folio Press
P. O. Box 2041
Grand Rapids, MI 49501-2041

ISBN 1-882701-26-7

Cover design by J. B. Nicholson, Jr.
Inset cover photo of Yemenite Jew ©1997 Richard Nowitz
http://www.nowitz.com

All Scripture quotations from the King James Version
unless otherwise noted.

Printed in the United States of America

Foreword

It would hardly be possible to overestimate the importance of a knowledge of God's dealings with Abraham and his seed for a proper understanding of the Bible. To him the Lord gave this sweeping promise, *"I will bless them that bless thee, and curse him that curseth thee: and in thee shall all families of the earth be blessed"* (Gen. 12:3). From Galatians 3:16 we learn that that seed was Christ, and in Him alone all the blessings of the New Covenant shall be realized. The significance of this subject in the Bible can be assessed by the fact that only a few chapters describe the creation of the worlds, while the rest of the Old Testament is largely dedicated to God's dealings with this one man and his family.

Abraham is also one of the most interesting characters of Bible history. There are few people mentioned so frequently in the Scriptures. Concordance pages show that besides the many, many places where his name appears in the Old Testament, he is mentioned more than seventy times in eleven books of the New Testament. He has the distinction of being called *"the Friend of God"* (Jas. 2:23).

To prepare Abraham for the place God had purposed for him, the God of glory appeared to him (Acts 7:2) and gave him wonderful visions—visions of the Lord Jesus (Jn. 8:56) and visions of a heavenly city *"which hath foundations, whose builder and maker is God"* (Heb. 11:10).

For the sake of continuity, the name "Abraham" is always used rather than sometimes "Abram" and at other times "Abraham," with the exception of scripture quotations which are left as the text designates.

There are two main themes emphasized in this book: the practical lessons we can learn from Abraham's life, and the devotional portraits we can see that give us glimpses of the *other* Father and His Son. First issued by Gospel Folio Press in 1957, we trust this new edition of *Abraham, the Friend of God* may continue to be blessed by the Lord, fulfilling in part the promise of God to Abraham that through him the nations of the world would be blessed.

THE PUBLISHERS
March, 2000

ABRAHAM'S GOD

The God of Abraham praise,
Who reigns enthroned above;
Ancient of everlasting days
And God of love:
Jehovah, great I AM,
By earth and heaven confessed,
I bow and bless the sacred Name,
Forever blessed.

The God of Abraham praise
At whose supreme command
From earth I rise to seek my joys
At His right hand.
He calls me to forsake
Earth's wisdom, fame and power,
And Him my only portion make,
My shield and tower.

The God of Abraham praise,
Whose all-sufficient grace
Shall guide me all my pilgrim days,
In all my ways.
He calls a worm His friend,
He calls Himself my God,
And He shall save me to the end,
Through Jesus' blood.

He by Himself hath sworn,
I on His oath depend,
I shall, on eagle wings upborne,
To heaven ascend:
I shall behold His face,
I shall His power adore,
And sing the wonders of His grace
For evermore.   —T. O.

Contents

ONE

On the Other Side of the River

Now these are the generations of Terah: Terah begat Abram, Nahor, and Haran; and Haran begat Lot. And Haran died before his father Terah in the land of his nativity, in Ur of the Chaldees. And Abram and Nahor took them wives: the name of Abram's wife was Sarai; and the name of Nahor's wife, Milcah, the daughter of Haran, the father of Milcah, and the father of Iscah. But Sarai was barren; she had no child. GENESIS 11:27-30

To understand and profit by the history of Abraham it is necessary to realize the character of the world in which he lived, and from which he was called.

THE BACKGROUND OF HIS LIFE

The Apostle Peter refers to the time before the flood as *"the world that then was."* The Apostle Paul speaks of *"this present evil world"* (Gal. 1:4); and finally, he speaks of *"the world to come"*—the Millennial world (Heb. 2:5). There is, then, the world that then was, the world that now is, and the world to come.

The world before the flood was ruined at the fall, and became utterly lawless. For sixteen hundred and fifty years God bore with the increasing wickedness of men, until the whole world—having become corrupt before God and filled with violence—reaped the judgment of God and *"the world that then was, being overflowed with water, perished"* (2 Pet. 3:6).

After the flood, the world that now is had its commencement. It was marked by entirely new elements. Government was introduced so that, in the mercy of God, wickedness should not go unpunished. Man was made responsible to curb evil by exercising judgment on the wicked. Noah was told, *"whoso sheddeth man's blood, by man shall his blood be shed."* But as man had failed in innocence and ruined the world before the flood, so man failed in government and ruined the present world.

As ever, when man is set in a place of responsibility, he fails, and that from the outset. Noah, who was set to govern, fails to govern himself. He became drunk and was mocked by his son. In the main, these things unfortunately have marked the government of the world. Those put in authority fail to govern, and those in opposition mock their failure.

Moreover, we see that, as time passed, men misused government to exalt themselves, and acted in independence of God. They say, *"Let us build us a city...and let us make us a name."* Finally the world became apostate and fell into idolatry, for we read, *"Thus saith the Lord God of Israel, Your fathers dwelt on the other side of the flood* [the river Euphrates] *in old time, even Terah, the father of Abraham, and the father of Nachor: and they served other gods"* (Josh. 24:2).

As a restraint upon man's evil, the world was separated into different families, with distinct nationalities and diverse languages. By this confounding of languages, knowledge was fragmented, thus limiting or delaying the damage that men could do with that knowledge.

Such then, was the commencement, and such is the character of the present evil world which is fast ripening for judgment. A world in which government is constituted by God, but ruined in the hands of men, who act independently of God, exalt themselves, and finally apostatize from God, falling into idolatry.

THE TURNING POINT IN ABRAHAM'S LIFE

For over four hundred years, God bore with this world. Then suddenly the God of glory appeared to a man on earth and commenced to act on an entirely new principle— that of the sovereign call of God. It does not set aside the government of the world; it makes no suggestion as to improving or reforming the world, or correcting its evil. It leaves the world just as it is, but it asserts God's paramount claim on an individual, who is elected in sovereign grace, and called out of the world. Abraham's call was to be the instrument of God's blessing to the nations of the world entirely apart from human government. Through his family would come both the written Word and the living Word that would introduce salvation to the whole world.

We cannot help but realize the importance of this great truth, when we see from the New Testament that it is still the principle on which God is acting today. The Church is entirely composed of individuals that are called by grace. The Apostle Paul clearly states that God has not only *"saved us"* but also *"called us"*; and that this calling is *"an holy calling...according to His own purpose"* (2 Tim. 1:9). Again, in his epistle to the Romans we are reminded that believers are *"the called according to His purpose"* (Rom. 8:28). So in writing to the Hebrew believers, the

Apostle appeals to them as *"partakers of the heavenly calling"* (Heb. 3:1). The Apostle Peter tells us we are *"called... out of darkness into His marvellous light,"* and, he adds, *"the God of all grace...hath called us unto His eternal glory"* (1 Pet. 2:9; 5:10).

It is clear then that believers are not only *"saved"* but *"called."* Naturally the first concern of an anxious soul is, like the Philippian jailer, *"What must I do to be saved?"* Having found salvation through faith in Christ and His finished work, we are too often content to rest in the knowledge that our sins are forgiven, that we are sheltered from judgment and saved from hell. We are slow to see that the same gospel that brings the good news of salvation from judgment proclaims the call of God to the glory of Christ. The Apostle says to the Thessalonian believers that God *"...called you by our gospel, to the obtaining of the glory of our Lord Jesus Christ"* (2 Thess. 2:13-14).

These different passages clearly show that if God calls us it is because He has a purpose in His heart which He desires to gratify. Moreover we learn that we are called out of one world lying in darkness, in ignorance of God, to come into the marvelous light of all that God has purposed for Christ in another world. Further, if we are called to heaven, it is that we may enter into the glory of our Lord Jesus Christ. The prize of the calling on high is to be *with* Christ and *like* Christ.

These are some of the blessed truths connected with the call of God and illustrated in the life of Abraham. The practical importance of the story of Abraham's life lies in the fact that this great truth of the calling of God is brought before us, not by a doctrinal statement, but as exhibited in the life of a man of like passions with ourselves. Thus the patriarch's life gives us a living, breathing portrait of what it means to be a friend of God.

TWO

The Call of God

And Terah took Abram his son, and Lot the son of Haran his son's son, and Sarai his daughter in law, his son Abram's wife; and they went forth with them from Ur of the Chaldees, to go into the land of Canaan; and they came unto Haran, and dwelt there. And the days of Terah were two hundred and five years: and Terah died in Haran. Now the Lord had said unto Abram, Get thee out of thy country, and from thy kindred, and from thy father's house, unto a land that I will show thee: And I will make of thee a great nation, and I will bless thee, and make thy name great; and thou shalt be a blessing: And I will bless them that bless thee, and curse him that curseth thee: and in thee shall all families of the earth be blessed. GENESIS 11:31-12:3

In the first period of Abraham's life we are introduced to the path of faith and those who walk there in answer to the call of God. We also see the hindrances on the path; the faith that takes the path; and the blessings in the path as well as the failure, temptations, and conflicts found there.

Let us think first of the character of the call by which the Lord began to woo Abraham from Ur to the city of God.

A DIVINE CALL

The first great truth we learn in the opening portion of Abraham's history is the blessed character of the call of God. From Stephen's address, recorded in Acts 7, we learn that *"The God of glory appeared unto our father Abraham, when he was in Mesopotamia."* What distinguishes the call from every other call is this: it comes from God—the God of glory. Human civilization, with its cities and towers reaching up to heaven, has nothing that speaks of God, only that which exalts and displays the glory of man. *"The God of glory"* speaks of another world in which there is nothing of man's self-aggrandizement but everything that displays the character of God. This is the God who in wonderful grace appears to a man living in a world estranged from God and steeped in idolatry.

So it is the glory of the One that appears to Abraham that gives such importance to the call, and gives faith its authority and power to answer to that call.

A SEPARATING CALL

Secondly, we learn that the call is a separating call. The word to Abraham is, *"Get thee out of thy country, and from thy kindred, and from thy father's house."* Abraham is not told to remain in the city of Ur and deal with man's wickedness, or attempt to improve its social condition, or reform its domestic ways, or attempt to make it a better and a brighter world. He is called to come out of it in every form. He is to leave the political world—*"thy country;"* the social world—*"thy kindred,"* and the domestic world—*"thy father's house."*

The call today is no less definite. The world around us is a world that has the form of godliness without the power—the world of corrupt religion; and the epistle that tells us that we are partakers of the heavenly calling exhorts us to separate from its corruption. We are to *"...go forth therefore unto Him* [Jesus] *without the camp, bearing His reproach"* (Heb. 13:13). It is not that we are to despise government—it is still God's appointment. We are instructed to pray for those in authority (1 Tim. 2:1-2), to refrain from speaking evil of dignitaries (2 Pet. 2:10; Jude 1:8), to pay our taxes (Mk. 12:17; Rom. 13:6-7), and to obey the laws of the land (Rom. 13:1-5).

Nor can we neglect family ties—they are ordered by God. Nor are we to cease to be courteous, and kind, and do good to all men as we have opportunity. But, as believers we are called from taking part in political activities of the world, the social round, and the whole sphere in which unconverted members of our families find their pleasure without God. We are not asked to reform the world or seek to improve its condition, but to come out from it. The word is still, *"Come out from among them, and be ye separate, saith the Lord, and touch not the unclean thing; and I will receive you, and will be a Father unto you, and ye shall be my sons and daughters, saith the Lord Almighty"* (2 Cor. 6:17-18).

AN ASSURING CALL

Thirdly, if the call of God separated Abraham from this present world, it is in view of bringing into another world *"a land,"* God said, *"that I will show thee."* If the God of glory appeared to Abraham, it was in order to bring Abraham into the glory of God. Thus the wonderful address of Stephen (Acts 7) that commences with the God of glory appearing to a man on earth (v. 2), ends with a Man appearing in the glory of God in heaven (v. 55). In closing his address, Stephen looked up steadfastly into heaven and saw the glory of God, and Jesus standing at the right hand of God, and he says, *"Behold, I see the heavens opened, and the Son of Man standing on the right hand of God."* Looking at Christ in glory, we see the wonderful purpose that God has in His heart when He calls us out of this present world. He has called us to glory, to be like Christ and with Christ in a scene where everything speaks of God and all that He is in the infinite love of His heart.

God does not say to Abraham, "If you answer to the call, I will immediately give you possession of the land." But He says, *"I will show thee the land."* If we answer His call, God allows us, along with Stephen, to *"see the King in His beauty"* and the land that is very far off ("of far distances," Isa. 33:17). We look up and see Christ in glory.

AN ADVANTAGEOUS CALL

There is great present blessing for the one who answers the call. As separated from this present evil world, God says to Abraham, *"I will make of thee a great nation, and I will bless thee, and make thy name great."* The men of this world seek to make a great name for themselves; they say, *"Let us make us a name."* But God says to the separated man, *"I will bless thee and make thy name great."*

The tendency of our natural hearts is always to seek to make a name for ourselves, and the flesh will seize on anything, even the things of God, to exalt itself. This tendency was seen even among the disciples of the Lord when they debated among themselves as to which of them should be accounted the greatest.

The scattering of man at Babel, and the divisions of Christendom, as well as every strife among the people of God, can be traced to this one root—the vanity of the flesh seeking to make itself great. *"Only by pride cometh contention"* (Prov. 13:10).

The lowly mind of the Lord Jesus led Him to make

Himself of no reputation. *"Wherefore God also hath highly exalted Him, and given Him a Name which is above every name."* God has made His Name great (Rev. 15:4), and to the one that has His lowly mind and follows Him outside the camp in answer to the call, God says, *"I will make thy name great."* God can make a much greater name for the believer in His world of glory than we can for ourselves in this present evil world.

If honestly confessed, it may well be found that the true motive for some Christians remaining in a soul-deadening religious system is the secret desire to be great. Thus they shrink from the path of obscurity outside the religious world. Can we not see in Scripture, as in daily experience, that those who have been spiritually great among the people of God have been separated—men and women who have answered the call of God; while any departure from the separated path has led to the loss of real influence and true spiritual greatness among the people of God?

A Beneficial Call

God says to Abraham, *"Thou shalt be a blessing."* In the path of separation, not only would Abraham himself be blessed, he would be a blessing to others. We do well to mark the import of these words. How often a believer remains in an association which he would admit is not according to the Word of God on the plea that he will be more useful to others than in the outside place of separation. However, God does not say to Abraham, "If you stop in Ur of the Chaldees, or in the halfway house at Haran you will be a blessing," but, answering to God's call he is told, *"Thou shalt be a blessing."* Perhaps Lot felt he could have influence sitting in the gate of Sodom, but the man who had influence there—who almost spared the city by his intercessions—was the man under the oak at Mamre.

A PRESERVING CALL

Sixthly, Abraham is told that in the outside place he would have the preserving care of God. He may indeed have to face opposition and trial, for it is ever true that *"he that departeth from evil maketh himself a prey"* (Isa. 59:15). But God says to the separated man, *"I will...curse him that curseth thee."* The separated man is preserved from many a trial that overtakes the believer who remains in association with the world. The mercy of the Lord saved Lot from the doom of Sodom, but, in that false association he lost everything—wife, family, wealth, and testimony.

AN EFFECTIVE CALL

Acting on faith in God's word, Abraham was told, *"In thee shall all families of the earth be blessed."* We know the use that the Spirit of God makes of this promise. He says, *"The scripture, foreseeing that God would justify the heathen* [on the principle] *of faith, preached before the gospel unto Abraham, saying, In thee shall all nations be blessed"* (Gal. 3:8). Abraham did not, and could not foresee the far-reaching effect of the principle of faith on which he acted in answering to the call of God, but God foresaw that it was the one way of blessing for all the families of the earth. So now none but God can foresee the far-reaching effect in blessing for others that may result when we, in simple and wholehearted faith, answer to the call of God.

THE HINDRANCE TO ANSWERING THE CALL OF GOD

We have seen the blessed promises that are connected with the call of God, and we shall learn how faith responds to the call. First, however, in this deeply instructive history, we are permitted to see how often the man of faith may be hindered for a time from answering to the call.

From Stephen's address, recorded in Acts 7, we learn that the call came to Abraham, *"when he was in Mesopotamia, before he dwelt in Charran."* In answering to this call he was hindered by the ties of nature. The call came to Abraham, but nature apparently can at times profess great zeal in answering the call, and even take the lead, for we read, *"Terah took Abram...and went forth from Ur of the Chaldees, to go into the land of Canaan."* Man in his natural state may attempt to tread the path of faith, and, at the start, do the right thing with the best of intentions. But in its self-confidence nature always undertakes to do more than it has the power to accomplish. Thus it came to pass that while Terah left Ur *"to go to the land of Canaan,"* he never reached the land. Nature stopped halfway at Haran, and there he dwelt to the day of his death.

But what of Abraham, the man of God? For a time he allowed himself to be hindered from fully obeying the call of God. It was not simply that his father was with him; he allowed himself to be led by his father, as we read, *"Terah took Abram."* The result being that he stopped short of the land to which he was called. So we read, in Stephen's address, he came *"out of the land of the Chaldaeans, and dwelt in Charran: and from thence, when his father was dead, he removed him into this land."*

How many of us have been hindered for a time from taking the separate path, consistent with the call of God, by some beloved relative. The call reaches the believer; he acknowledges the truth, but delays to answer it because some near relative is not prepared for the outside place. The soul clings to the hope that by waiting a little the relative will be brought to see the call, and then both can act together. Faith, however, cannot lift nature up to its own level, though, alas, nature can drag down and hinder the man of faith. Many pleas can be raised to excuse this halfway halt, but in reality it is putting the claims of nature above the call of God. Then, as in Abraham's history, God may have to roll death into the family circle and remove the one that we allowed to hinder us in obeying God's call. Thus it was not until his father was dead that Abraham fully answered to the call of God.

To walk with God! O fellowship Divine!
Man's highest state on earth—Lord, be it mine!
With Thee may I a close communion hold,
To Thee the deep recesses of my heart unfold.

Yes, tell Thee all—each weary care and grief
Into Thy bosom pour, till there I find relief.
Oh! let me walk with Thee, Thou Mighty One!
Lean on Thine arm, and trust Thy love alone.

My every comfort at Thy hand receive,
My every talent to Thy glory give.
Thy counsel seek in every trying hour,
In all my weakness trust Thy mighty power.

Oh! may this high companionship be mine,
And all my life by its reflection shine.
My great, my wise, my never-failing Friend,
Whose love no change can know, no turn, no end!

THREE

Faith and Unbelief

So Abram departed, as the Lord had spoken unto him; and Lot went with him: and Abram was seventy and five years old when he departed out of Haran. And Abram took Sarai his wife, and Lot his brother's son, and all their substance that they had gathered, and the souls that they had gotten in Haran; and they went forth to go into the land of Canaan; and into the land of Canaan they came. And Abram passed through the land unto the place of Sichem, unto the plain of Moreh. And the Canaanite was then in the land. And the Lord appeared unto Abram, and said, Unto thy seed will I give this land: and there builded he an altar unto the Lord, who appeared unto him. And he removed from thence unto a mountain on the east of Bethel, and pitched his tent, having Bethel on the west, and Hai on the east: and there he builded an altar unto the Lord, and called upon the name of the Lord. And Abram journeyed, going on still toward the south. And there was a famine in the land: and Abram went down into Egypt to sojourn there; for the famine was grievous in the land. And it came to pass, when he was come near to enter into Egypt, that he said unto Sarai his wife, Behold now, I know that thou art a fair woman to look upon: Therefore it shall come to pass, when the Egyptians shall see thee, that they shall say, This is his wife: and they will kill me, but they will save thee alive. Say, I pray thee, thou art my sister: that it may be well with me for thy sake; and my soul shall live because of thee. And it came to pass, that, when Abram was come into Egypt, the Egyptians beheld the woman that she was very fair. The princes also of Pharaoh saw her, and commended her before Pharaoh: and the woman was taken into Pharaoh's house. And he entreated Abram well for her sake: and he had sheep, and oxen, and he asses, and menservants, and maidservants, and she asses, and camels. And the Lord plagued Pharaoh and his house with great plagues because of Sarai Abram's wife. And Pharaoh called Abram, and said, What is this that thou hast done unto me? why didst thou not tell me that she was thy wife? Why saidst thou, She is my sister? so I might have taken her to me to wife: now therefore behold thy wife, take her, and go thy way. And Pharaoh commanded his men concerning him: and they sent him away, and his wife, and all that he had. Genesis 12:4-20

Abraham had been set free from the ties of nature, though at the painful cost of death coming into the family circle. After his father was removed by death, Abraham obeyed the call, as we read, *"So Abram departed as the Lord had spoken unto him."*

He took Lot, his nephew, with him, and Lot with his worldly-mindedness would prove an encumbrance to him. In the case of his father, Abraham who was called allowed nature to lead, for *"Terah took Abram,"* and this became a deadly hindrance. In the case of the nephew, Abraham took the lead, for we read *"Abram took...Lot,"* and therefore, while this might become a weight, it did not hinder faith answering the call.

When nature took the lead, we read, *"They went forth...from Ur of the Chaldees, to go into the land of Canaan."* But they never reach the land under the leading of Terah. Now, when faith takes the lead we again read, *"They went forth to go into the land of Canaan; and into the land of Canaan they came"* (v. 5).

A CONTRAST

Arriving in Canaan, they found *"the Canaanite was then in the land."* This is deeply significant. Of Abraham, God had said, *"I will bless thee."* Of Canaan, God had said, *"Cursed be Canaan."* God brought Abraham—the man of blessing—into the land of promise, but he at once discovered that the devil had already brought into that very land the man of the curse. In this way the devil sought to thwart the purpose of God, and hinder the man of faith from entering into possession of the land.

A COMPARISON

So it is with the Christian. He is called out of the present world, he is a partaker of the heavenly calling, he is blessed with all spiritual blessings in heavenly places. But, answering to the call and leaving the world, he finds that he is opposed by *"spiritual wickedness in high places"* (Eph. 6:12). The believer that seeks to enter into his spiritual blessings will find there is arrayed against him spiritual wickedness seeking to prevent him from taking the heavenly ground that is the only true portion of the Church.

For Abraham, Ur was in the past; the possession of the land was yet future. In the meantime he had neither the world that he had left, nor the better world to which he was going. This, too, is the position of the Christian who answers the call of God. He has left this present evil world and he has not yet reached the world to come.

What then, we may ask, is the portion of the one who answers the call, and what will sustain him in this place outside the present world order and not yet enjoying the world to come? Here the story of Abraham is rich with instruction and encouragement.

THE OBEDIENCE OF FAITH

First note that the great principle on which Abraham acted was the principle of faith. Obviously, if he had left one world, and had not reached the other, he had nothing for natural sight. It is not that he did not see, but, what he saw was by faith. Thus we read, *"By faith Abraham, when he was called to go out into a place which he should after receive for an inheritance, obeyed";* and, again; *"By faith he sojourned in the land of promise."* He and his own lived by faith, and finally we read, *"These all died in faith"* (Heb. 11:8-9, 13).

THE PATH OF FAITH

Answering the call of God on faith, Abraham and those with him became *"strangers and pilgrims."* As the Holy Spirit in the New Testament can say of them, they *"confessed that they were strangers and pilgrims on the earth"* (Heb. 11:13). This comes before us very strikingly in his history. In Haran, where Abraham was detained for a time, we read, he *"dwelt there";* but when he arrived in the land, we read he *"pitched his tent"* as one that had no certain dwelling place. Moreover, we read that he *"passed through the land."* As a stranger he had only a tent in this world; as a pilgrim he was passing through to another world.

THE PORTION OF FAITH

Thirdly, we learn what sustained Abraham in this pilgrim path. We are told, *"The Lord appeared unto Abram, and said, Unto thy seed will I give this land."* Mark well these two things. First, the twice repeated statement *"the Lord appeared"* to him; secondly, the land was set before him as a future possession. He pursued his journey as a stranger and a pilgrim in the light of the glory of the God who had called him, and the blessedness of the land to which he was going. So we read in the New Testament, *"He looked for a city which hath foundations,"* and again, he looked for *"a better country, that is, an heavenly"* (Heb. 11:10, 16).

Nor is it otherwise with ourselves. It is only as we have Christ Himself before us in His glory and the blessedness of the heavenly home to which we are going that we shall, in any measure, bear the stranger and pilgrim character. It is not enough to know the doctrine of Christ, and that heaven lies before us at the end of the journey, but, like the Apostle, the desire of each heart should be, *"That I may know Him,"* and *"apprehend that for which also I am apprehended of Christ Jesus"* (Phil. 3:10, 12).

Taking a place outside this world order in answer to the call, it is possible to grow in our personal acquaintance with the Lord Himself, for He has said, *"He that hath My commandments, and keepeth them, he it is that loveth Me: and he that loveth Me shall be loved of My Father, and I will love him, and will manifest Myself to him."*

The Response of Faith

After the Lord appeared to Abraham, we immediately read, *"There builded he an altar."* This surely speaks of worship. In the Epistle to the Hebrews those who *"go forth"* to Christ outside the camp not only take up their pilgrim character as having no continuing city, but they become worshippers who *"offer the sacrifice of praise to God continually"* (Heb. 13:13-15).

Abraham not only realized something of the glory of the

land in the far future, but he caught a glimpse of the glory of the One that had appeared to him. The gift of the land might well call forth his thanksgiving, but the blessedness of the Giver made him a worshipper. This always happens, for worship is the outflow of a heart that is filled with the glory of the Person we adore.

RESOURCE OF FAITH

Fifthly, Abraham *"called upon the Name of the Lord."* This speaks of dependence on the Lord. Whatever his needs, whatever the privations of his pilgrim journey, whatever opposition he may have to meet, whatever temptations might cross his path, he had an unfailing resource—he could call on the Name of the Lord.

In every day of difficulty the godly find their resource in the Lord. In the day of ruin before the flood there were those who, like Cain, *"went out from the presence of the Lord"*; but, there were also the godly who *"began...to call upon the Name of the Lord"* (Gen. 4:16, 26). So in the dark days of Malachi the godly found their resource in the Lord, for we read, they *"thought upon His Name"* (Mal. 3:16). In the early days of the Church, believers were known as those who *"called on this Name"* (Acts 9:21). In the midst of their persecutions it was to the Lord that they turned. And in the midst of the ruin of these last days, we are assured that there will be still those *"that call on the Lord out of a pure heart"* (2 Tim. 2:22).

However striking the faith of Abraham, we are made to realize that he is a man of like passions with ourselves. No one takes the path of faith without being tested. The test is allowed to uncover to us on the one hand our weakness, and on the other the grace and faithfulness of God, *"So that we may boldly say, The Lord is my helper, and I will not fear what man shall do unto me"* (Heb. 13:6).

THE FAITHLESSNESS OF ABRAHAM

In Abraham's history the test came in the form of a famine. It was a severe test for *"the famine was grievous in the land."* If the Lord allowed the famine, the Lord could surely meet the needs of His own in the famine. However, under the pressure of his need, Abraham allowed the circumstances to come between his soul and the Lord. Instead of calling on the Lord, he followed the dictates of mere reason, or common sense, and, for a time, stepped out of the path of faith and *"went down into Egypt."* Instead of counting on God to sustain him, he went to the world for help.

Having taken this false step, he found that though his immediate needs were met, he was faced with fresh difficulties occasioned by his false position. He feared that he would be killed in order to satisfy the lusts of Egypt.

Having taken a position in which he could no longer count on God to preserve him, he was left to his own resources to meet this fresh difficulty. He sank below the level of the world and acted a lie. With this equivocation he sought to protect himself at the expense of his wife.

Unbelief, carrying its own judgment, constantly leads into the very evil one seeks to avoid. As it has been said, *"The sons of men would build a tower lest they should be scattered abroad, and the Lord scattered them because they built it. Abram, fearing lest Pharaoh should take his wife, says she is his sister (as if God would not preserve him), and therefore Pharaoh takes her into his house"* (J. N. DARBY). So again, at a later day in similar circumstances, Elimelech left the land of God in order to escape the fear of death by famine, only to find that death awaited him in the land of Moab (Ruth 1:1-5).

By this false step, Abraham found relief from his immediate need, and even acquired riches, but at what a cost. For in Egypt he could pitch no tent and raise no altar, nor call on the Name of the Lord.

THE FAITHFULNESS OF ABRAHAM'S GOD

Yet in spite of failure, God is faithful to His own. The gifts and calling of God are without repentance. God does not give up His people when they break down. He acts on our behalf, though we have to suffer for our folly. Thus it was that God acted on behalf of his failing servant. We read, *"the Lord plagued Pharaoh and his house with great plagues because of Sarai Abram's wife."*

In result, when the deceit was discovered, Abraham was dismissed by the world, for Pharaoh says, *"Behold thy wife, take her, and go thy way."* And Pharaoh took care that he did go, for he *"commanded his men concerning him: and they sent him away, and his wife, and all that he had."* Alas when the world dismisses the people of God, not because of their faithful witness to God, but because of their own shameful conduct! Thus, in the goodness of God, His poor servant Abraham was set free from a false position, but not without reproach and shame.

Oh, what is all that earth can give?
I'm called to share in God's own joy.
Dead to the world, in Thee I live,
In Thee I've bliss without alloy:
Well may I earthly things resign;
"All things" are mine, and I am Thine!

Till Thou shalt come to take me home,
Be this my one ambition, Lord,
Self, sin, the world, to overcome,
Fast clinging to Thy faithful Word:
More of Thyself each day to know,
And more into Thine image grow.

FOUR

Refusing and Choosing

And Abram went up out of Egypt, he, and his wife, and all that he had, and Lot with him, into the south. And Abram was very rich in cattle, in silver, and in gold. And he went on his journeys from the south even to Bethel, unto the place where his tent had been at the beginning, between Bethel and Hai; unto the place of the altar, which he had made there at the first: and there Abram called on the name of the Lord. And Lot also, which went with Abram, had flocks, and herds, and tents. And the land was not able to bear them, that they might dwell together: for their substance was great, so that they could not dwell together. And there was a strife between the herdmen of Abram's cattle and the herdmen of Lot's cattle: and the Canaanite and the Perizzite dwelled then in the land. And Abram said unto Lot, Let there be no strife, I pray thee, between me and thee, and between my herdmen and thy herdmen; for we be brethren. Is not the whole land before thee? Separate thyself, I pray thee, from me: if thou wilt take the left hand, then I will go to the right; or if thou depart to the right hand, then I will go to the left. And Lot lifted up his eyes, and beheld all the plain of Jordan, that it was well watered everywhere, before the Lord destroyed Sodom and

> *Gomorrah, even as the garden of the Lord, like the land of Egypt, as thou comest unto Zoar. Then Lot chose all the plain of Jordan; and Lot journeyed east: and they separated themselves the one from the other. Abram dwelled in the land of Canaan, and Lot dwelled in the cities of the plain, and pitched his tent toward Sodom. But the men of Sodom were wicked and sinners before the Lord exceedingly.*
>
> *And the Lord said unto Abram, after that Lot was separated from him, Lift up now thine eyes, and look from the place where thou art northward, and southward, and eastward, and westward: for all the land which thou seest, to thee will I give it, and to thy seed for ever. And I will make thy seed as the dust of the earth: so that if a man can number the dust of the earth, then shall thy seed also be numbered. Arise, walk through the land in the length of it and in the breadth of it; for I will give it unto thee. Then Abram removed his tent, and came and dwelt in the plain of Mamre, which is in Hebron, and built there an altar unto the Lord.*　　　　　　　　　　　　　　GENESIS 13

The reality of Abraham's restoration to the path of faith was speedily put to the test. Circumstances arose that manifested he was once again living in the light of the heavenly country, and could therefore afford to refuse the well-watered plain chosen by his worldly-minded nephew.

RECOVERY FROM FAILURE

Abraham had been dismissed from Egypt. Where he went was a matter of indifference to the world. Abraham, however, was a true man of faith, though like ourselves he at times broke down in the path of faith. Having tasted the blessedness of the outside place, nothing would satisfy his soul but getting back into the place of blessing from which his feet had strayed. So we read, *"Abram went up out of*

Egypt...into the south...and he went on his journeys from the south even to Bethel, unto the place where his tent had been...unto the place of the altar" (Gen. 13:1-4).

As with every truly restored soul, he retraced his path step by step until, once again, he was found in his stranger and pilgrim character with his tent, as a worshipper with his altar, and as a dependent man calling on the Name of the Lord.

THE RESULT OF FAILURE

Abraham's restoration was complete; but the result of Abraham's failure is seen in others. A saint never fails without affecting others for evil, though he himself may be restored. The effect of his failure on Lot at once comes to light. In Terah we have seen the man of nature who can make a fair profession, but cannot take the path of faith that leads outside the world. In Abraham, we have seen the man of faith who, acting according to the word of the Lord, takes the outside place, though at times he may fail in this path. In Lot we see a true believer who takes the outside place, not in faith in God but under the influence of man. Already we have read that when Abraham departed from Haran, *"Lot went with him"* (12:4). Again, when Abraham went up out of Egypt, we read, *"Lot with him"* (13:1). Now, for the third time Lot is described as the man *"which went with Abram."*

Lot represents a large class who take up a right position outside the world, but do so under the influence of a friend or relative rather than from personal exercise and faith in God. From the beginning of his path, Lot was characterized by walking in the light of another. Alas, in different ways and measures, how often we may, like Lot, act with those who have faith without having it ourselves, only to find that we shall not stand when tried by temptation.

When the test comes, believers who walk in the light of another will break down and give up a path which has no attraction for the flesh, about which they never had any exercise, and for which they have no personal faith.

THE SNARE OF RICHES

How often, too, the test today takes the form that it did in the story of Abraham and Lot. As we read, *"there was a strife."* We learn further that the immediate cause of the strife was their possessions. We do well to notice the twice-repeated statement that they were not able to dwell together, and the deeply significant cause of the division, *"for their substance was great."* How often since then believers have been divided by jealousy of one another's spiritual gifts or temporal riches. The abuse of spiritual gifts was a source of division in the assembly at Corinth. The apostle writes to this assembly, *"In everything ye are enriched by Him, in all utterance and in all knowledge."* But these very riches became a cause of strife and division, for, says the apostle, *"There is among you envying, and strife, and divisions";* and he adds that they were *"puffed up for one against another"* (1 Cor. 1:5; 3:3; 4:6). Poverty might have led them to cling to one another; their riches became a cause of division.

In the case of Abraham and Lot their temporal riches became the occasion of division. We may well ask, "Where were these temporal riches acquired?" When first Abraham entered on the path of faith, and Lot went with him, they took *"all their substance."* But it was no cause of strife (12:5). In Egypt, however, Abraham acquired great wealth so that after his restoration we read, He *"was **very rich** in cattle, in silver, and in gold"* (13:2).

The wealth that he acquired through turning aside from the path of faith became a cause of strife and division between brethren. Striving together, these brothers ceased to be a witness to God before the Canaanites and the Perizzites that dwelled in the land.

THE POSITION OF FAITH

Nevertheless, Abraham was a restored man in a true position with a right motive. Lot, though in a right position, was only a follower of others. Therefore, while strife became the sad occasion of revealing the worldly-mindedness of Lot, it also brought to light the heavenly-mindedness of Abraham, who was able to renounce things seen. Abraham says, *"Let there be no strife thee, I pray thee, between me and thee...for we be brethren."* The man who has no faith for the position where he finds himself will in the end become a source of strife among brethren. He had better separate from the man whose faith he cannot follow.

Abraham, with the heavenly country before him, could afford to renounce the present world with its prospect of ease and plenty. Lot could choose; and if he took the best according to nature and sight, Abraham would be content to take the path that God chose for him, be it rough or smooth, knowing that it would end in the land of promise with all its blessedness.

THE CHOICE OF THE FLESH

Under the influence of others, Lot had accepted the outside path: left to his own choice he showed that the world was in his heart (vv. 10-13). Without seeking direction from God, he chose his path according to sight. *"Lot lifted up his eyes and beheld all the the plain of Jordan."* It was an alluring sight and had promise of present ease and plenty. Everywhere there was water for his flocks, without the labor of digging wells. So fruitful was the plain that it was *"even as the garden of the Lord."* Most significant of all, it was *"like the land of Egypt."* Alas! Lot having followed Abraham into Egypt had acquired a taste for Egypt's pleasures and thus had strengthened the desire for worldly ease and plenty.

So Lot chose all the plain of Jordan, gave up the separate path for which he never had personal faith, and forever left the land of Canaan. There was nothing gross or wrong in choosing a well-watered plain; but it proved that the heart was not set on the unseen land of God's promise. Moreover, the real danger of the well-watered plains was that Satan had reared Sodom in their midst.

Abraham remained in the land of Canaan, and Lot dwelt in the cities of the plain. Having left the path of faith and chosen the path of sight and worldly ease, his way was always downward, for we next read that he *"pitched his tent toward Sodom."* Of this city we are told, *"The men of Sodom were wicked and sinners before the Lord exceedingly."* We shall yet learn that for Lot there was no recovery. Lower and lower he sank, until at last he passed from the scene under a cloud of shame and dishonor.

THE CONFESSION OF FAITH

Abraham, freed from the encumbrance of his worldly-minded nephew, received fresh communications from the Lord. Lot had allowed himself to be guided by the sight of his eyes apart from the direction of the Lord. The result was that the sight of his eyes stirred the lust of his heart, and his feet followed the choice of his heart.

Now Abraham used his eyes, but at the direction of the Lord, for, when Lot was separated from him, the Lord said, *"Lift up now thine eyes, and look from the place where thou art."* He was to look in every direction at the land which the Lord had given him. And so it will be for us. When freed from the weight of those who have no faith for the outside path, if we too set our minds on things above and *"look not at the things which are seen, but at the things which are not seen"* (2 Cor. 4:18), we will enjoy every part of the revelation that God has given to us of the world to come, the heavenly country with its city which has foundations.

In this sense, we can still answer to the Lord's direction to Abraham when He said, *"Arise, walk through the land in the length of it and in the breadth of it, for I will give it unto thee."* Set free from mere followers, rising above all petty strife and allowing the Lord to choose his path, Abraham enjoyed a rich unfolding of the world to come for which in patience he waited. In the meantime he moved through the land with his tent and his altar.

> *This world is a wilderness wide,*
> *I have nothing to seek or to choose;*
> *I've no thought in the waste to abide;*
> *I have nought to regret nor to lose.*
>
> *The Lord is Himself gone before;*
> *He has marked out the path that I tread:*
> *It's as sure as the love I adore;*
> *I have nothing to fear nor to dread.*
>
> *'Tis the treasure I've found in His love*
> *That has made me a pilgrim below;*
> *And 'tis there, when I reach Him above,*
> *As I'm known, all His fullness I'll know.*
>
> *Till then, 'tis the path Thou hast trod,*
> *My delight and my comfort shall be:*
> *I'm content with Thy staff and Thy rod,*
> *'Till with Thee all Thy glory I see.* —J. N. D.

FIVE

Victory and Defeat

*And it came to pass in the days of Amraphel king of Shinar,
Arioch king of Ellasar, Chedorlaomer king of Elam, and
Tidal king of nations; that these made war with Bera king
of Sodom, and with Birsha king of Gomorrah, Shinab king
of Admah, and Shemeber king of Zeboiim, and the king of
Bela, which is Zoar. All these were joined together in the
vale of Siddim, which is the salt sea. Twelve years they
served Chedorlaomer, and in the thirteenth year they
rebelled. And in the fourteenth year came Chedorlaomer,
and the kings that were with him...And there went out the
king of Sodom, and the king of Gomorrah, and the king of
Admah, and the king of Zeboiim, and the king of Bela (the
same is Zoar;) and they joined battle with them in the vale
of Siddim...four kings with five. And the vale of Siddim was
full of slimepits; and the kings of Sodom and Gomorrah
fled, and fell there; and they that remained fled to the
mountain. And they took all the goods of Sodom and
Gomorrah, and all their victuals, and went their way. And
they took Lot, Abram's brother's son, who dwelt in Sodom,
and his goods, and departed.*

*And there came one that had escaped, and told Abram
the Hebrew; for he dwelt in the plain of Mamre the*

Amorite, brother of Eshcol, and brother of Aner: and these were confederate with Abram. And when Abram heard that his brother was taken captive, he armed his trained servants, born in his own house, three hundred and eighteen, and pursued them unto Dan. And he divided himself against them, he and his servants, by night, and smote them, and pursued them unto Hobah, which is on the left hand of Damascus. And he brought back all the goods, and also brought again his brother Lot, and his goods, and the women also, and the people.

And the king of Sodom went out to meet him after his return from the slaughter of Chedorlaomer, and of the kings that were with him, at the valley of Shaveh, which is the king's dale. And Melchizedek king of Salem brought forth bread and wine: and he was the priest of the most high God. And he blessed him, and said, Blessed be Abram of the most high God, possessor of heaven and earth: and blessed be the most high God, which hath delivered thine enemies into thy hand. And he gave him tithes of all.

And the king of Sodom said unto Abram, Give me the persons, and take the goods to thyself. And Abram said to the king of Sodom, I have lift up mine hand unto the Lord, the most high God, the possessor of heaven and earth, That I will not take from a thread even to a shoelatchet, and that I will not take any thing that is thine, lest thou shouldest say, I have made Abram rich: save only that which the young men have eaten, and the portion of the men which went with me, Aner, Eshcol, and Mamre; let them take their portion.   GENESIS 14

In Genesis 12, we traced the blessedness of the path of faith in answering the call of God, and how our steps can slip unless held by the power of the Lord. In chapter 13, we saw the renunciation of the world by the believer who reads the path of faith; and, in contrast, the sorrowful choice of the world by the believer who allows himself to be governed by sight.

Now chapter 14 presents the conflicts of the world—nations warring against nations—during which the believer, who has refused the world, obtains the victory; while the believer, who walks by sight, falls under its power. Further we learn that the world's conflicts will finally issue through the judgments of God in the deliverance of God's people and the establishment of the reign of Christ as Priest and King. This is typically set forth in Melchizedek, king of Salem.

CONFLICT (vv. 1-11)

The chapter opens with a solemn picture of this present evil world. It is a scene in which the nations form themselves into groups, and enter into alliances to carry out their schemes of aggrandizement, and to defend themselves from attacks. Moreover, it was a lawless world where men were forced to serve governments against their will, or rebel against governments to obtain their liberty (v. 4).

Thus the whole world, whether in high places or in lower spheres—the mount or the wilderness (v. 6)—became a scene of warring interests, and selfish conflicts.

CAPTURE (v. 12)

The account of these world conflicts leads to what is so deeply instructive—the contrast between the believer who is governed by sight, and the one who walks by faith. In the course of these conflicts, Lot, the man of sight, fell a captive to the world; Abraham, the man of faith, was victorious over the world.

Thus we read that the victorious kings *"took Lot, Abram's brother's son, who dwelt in Sodom, and his goods, and departed."* It is significant to notice that Lot, of whom we read in a former chapter, chose all the plain of Jordan, and *"pitched his tent toward Sodom"* (13:12), has taken a further step on his downward course. Here we read he *"dwells in Sodom."* We may be sure that it was never Lot's intention to dwell in Sodom, when he pitched his tent toward Sodom, but one false step leads to another. Drawing near to the world, he was soon in the world; and dwelling in the world he became involved in its conflicts, and fell a captive to its power.

It is still true that the believer who settles down in the world has no power against the world. Where there is not the faith that keeps the coming of glory in view, there is not the faith to overcome the present evil world. This was the case of Lot. He never overcame, but was constantly overcome by one evil influence after another. He accepted the outside path under the leading of Abraham rather than of faith in God. When the test came, he fell under the influence of fair prospects that appealed to the sight of the eyes. Having drawn near to the world, he fell still further under its influence, and settled down in Sodom. Finally, dwelling in Sodom, he found in the day of conflict he was a lonely man, without strength, without friends to help, and unable to count on the support of God. Powerless in the day of battle, he fell captive to his enemies.

CONTRAST (VV. 13-16)

In contrast to Lot, who chose the world and became its captive, there is presented before us the man who renounced the world and was victorious over it. Lot, as we have seen, was unprepared in the day of battle; Abraham, dwelling as one apart, was ready for conflict. He had in his household those who had already been trained for conflict, and he was ready to fight the good fight—not, like the world for personal aggrandizement, or to obtain the riches of this world, but to rescue a brother who had fallen under its power.

The weapons of our warfare are not carnal, and we do not wrestle against flesh and blood. Nonetheless, the Christian conflict is very real. We contend for the truth, and seek to deliver those who are in danger of falling into the world, or have already been taken captive in its toils.

Paul, living in the light of another world and glorying in the cross of our Lord Jesus Christ, by whom the world was crucified to Paul and he to it, fought the good fight and escaped the snare of those who would be rich whereby they pierced themselves through with many sorrows. He had great conflict for those who were in danger of falling under the power of the religious world (Col. 2:1).

Likewise Jude, in the spirit of Abraham, hating even the garment spotted by the flesh, was ready earnestly to contend for the faith. Such can have compassion on those believers who have been taken captive by the world, and seek to pull them out of the fire (Jude 1:3, 22-23).

COMPENSATION (VV. 17-24)

Abraham was not only victorious over the hostility of the world, he is proof against its horrors and its gifts. We may rise above the world's enmity, and yet fall beneath its kindness. And we are never more in danger of a fall than in the moment of victory. This the enemy knows full well and so comes with his temptations at a moment when we may be off guard. Thus with Abraham, *"the king of Sodom went out to meet Abram after his return"* from his triumph over the opposing kings. But if the king of Sodom came to tempt Abraham, the king of Salem was there to support him.

In the Epistle to the Hebrews, the Holy Spirit has given

us the spiritual significance of this fine scene. There Melchizedek is introduced as a type to set forth the glories of Christ. His name, and that of his country, signify that he was King of Righteousness and King of Peace. Moreover, he was *"the priest of the Most High God"* (see Heb. 7:1-3). As a king, he brought righteousness and peace to his subjects; as a priest, he led the praises of his people to God. As the representative of God before man, Melchizedek blessed Abraham on behalf of God; as the representative of man before God, he blessed the Most High God on behalf of Abraham.

Thus, in the coming Millennial days, God will be known as the Most High, who will deliver His earthly people from their enemies and deal in judgment with every hostile power. Then Christ will indeed shine forth as King and Priest. So we are told by direct prophecy, *"He shall bear the glory, and shall sit and rule upon His throne; and He shall be a priest upon His throne: and the counsel of peace shall be between them both"* (Zech. 6:13). He will be the true King of Righteousness, the King of Peace, and the Priest of the Most High God.

Melchizedek having brought forth bread and wine, the needs of Abraham were met and his joy secured, and thus he was strengthened to dispense with the gifts of this world. Abraham had lifted up his hand unto the Lord, the Most High God, the one who possesses all the fullness of heaven and earth. Blessed by God, he would take nothing from the world lest it should say, *"I have made Abram rich."*

Blessed with all spiritual blessings in heavenly places, and enriched with the unsearchable riches of Christ, the believer can rise above the seductions of this world, refuse its gifts and honors, and pursue in peace the life of faith in the path of separation. And faith treads this path in the light of the world to come. Faith knows that all the conflicts of this world will come to their end in the glorious reign of Christ, when His poor, failing people will be delivered from all their enemies, and righteousness and peace will be established, as we read, *"He shall judge Thy people with righteousness, and Thy poor with judgment. The mountains shall bring peace to the people"* (Ps. 72:2-3).

Father, Thy sovereign love has sought
Captives to sin, gone far from Thee:
The work that Thine own Son has wrought
Has brought us back in peace and free;
And now as sons before Thy face,
With joyful steps the path we tread,
Which leads us on to that bright place
Prepared for us by Christ our Head.

Thou gav'st us in eternal love
To Him to bring us home to Thee,
Suited to Thine own thought above,
As sons like Him, with Him, to be
In Thine own house. There love divine
Fills the bright courts with cloudless joy;
But 'tis the love that made us Thine,
Fills all that house without alloy.

O boundless grace! what fills with joy
Unmingled all who enter there,
God's nature, love without alloy,
Our hearts are given e'en now to share.
God's righteousness with glory bright,
Which with its radiance fills that sphere,
E'en Christ, of God the power and light,
Our title is that light to share.

O mind divine, so must it be
That glory all belongs to God:
O Love divine, that did decree
We should be part, thro' Jesus' blood.
O keep us, Love divine, near Thee,
That we our nothingness may know,
And ever to Thy glory be
Walking in faith while here below.

SIX

Sonship and Inheritance

After these things the word of the Lord came unto Abram in a vision, saying, Fear not, Abram: I am thy shield, and thy exceeding great reward. And Abram said, Lord God, what wilt Thou give me, seeing I go childless, and the steward of my house is this Eliezer of Damascus? And Abram said, Behold, to me Thou hast given no seed: and, lo, one born in my house is mine heir. And, behold, the word of the Lord came unto him, saying, This shall not be thine heir; but he that shall come forth out of thine own bowels shall be thine heir. And He brought him forth abroad, and said, Look now toward heaven, and tell the stars, if thou be able to number them: and He said unto him, So shall thy seed be. And he believed in the Lord; and He counted it to him for righteousness.

And He said unto him, I am the Lord that brought thee out of Ur of the Chaldees, to give thee this land to inherit it. And he said, Lord God, whereby shall I know that I shall inherit it? And He said unto him, Take Me an heifer of three years old, and a she goat of three years old, and a ram of three years old, and a turtledove, and a young pigeon. And he took unto Him all these, and divided them in the midst, and laid each piece one against another: but the birds divided he not. And when the fowls came down upon the carcasses, Abram drove them away. And when the sun was going down, a deep sleep fell upon Abram; and, lo, an horror of great darkness fell upon him.

And He said unto Abram, Know of a surety that thy seed shall be a stranger in a land that is not theirs, and shall serve them; and they shall afflict them four hundred years; and also that nation, whom they shall serve, will I judge: and afterward shall they come out with great substance. And thou shalt go to thy fathers in peace; thou shalt be buried in a good old age. But in the fourth generation they shall come hither again: for the iniquity of the Amorites is not yet full.

And it came to pass, that, when the sun went down, and it was dark, behold a smoking furnace, and a burning lamp that passed between those pieces. In the same day the Lord made a covenant with Abram, saying, Unto thy seed have I given this land, from the river of Egypt unto the great river, the river Euphrates: the Kenites, and the Kenizzites, and the Kadmonites, and the Hittites, and the Perizzites, and the Rephaims, and the Amorites, and the Canaanites, and the Girgashites, and the Jebusites. Genesis 15

In chapters 11–14, we saw the public witness of Abraham before men. In the second portion of his history, presented in chapters 15–21, we have the personal exercises of his soul before God. It is clear that Abraham's departure from Haran, his tent, his altar, his renunciation of the world, and his victory over the kings, were all matters of public knowledge, setting forth the life of faith and the glorious end to which it leads. Now we are to learn his inner exercises that lie behind his public testimony.

It is of the deepest moment to realize we are not merely

called to be witnesses of facts that are true, but to testify of truths that have affected our own souls.

In these marvelous scenes there is personal communion between God and a man of like passion with ourselves. God appeared to Abraham in visions and by personal visits, in which He talked with him and even accepted his hospitality. In these communications God revealed the purpose of His heart concerning Abraham and his posterity and, as a friend, disclosed His mind concerning the world.

THE REVELATION OF GOD (V. 1)

Abraham, on his side, could with full confidence spread out his needs before God, acknowledge all his difficulties, and plead for others. Such condescending grace on the part of God, and confiding trust on the part of Abraham, is deeply instructive to us. In the light of the full revelation of God as our Father, it is possible for believers to enjoy yet greater intimacy with God, though we may not hear His audible voice or sit by Him at the tent door. We may well challenge our hearts as to how much we know of this blessed intimacy that, in all the sweet confidence of children, can bring every difficulty to God, spread out our needs before Him, and, in the confidence of love, plead on behalf of others. We are at least encouraged by these lovely scenes to cultivate this intimacy with God.

The occasion of these fresh communications is deeply instructive. Abraham had just refused this world's gifts and honors. Now we read, *"After these things the word of the Lord came to Abram in a vision, saying, Fear not, Abram: I am thy shield, and thy exceeding great reward."* Having aroused the enmity of the world over whom he had gained a victory, he needed a shield. Having refused the gifts of this world, he had the rewards of God. And God's protection and God's rewards far exceed all that this world can offer. With God for our shield, we need not fear the reprisals of defeated enemies; with God for our reward, we can dispense with this world's gifts.

THE RESPONSE OF FAITH (VV. 2-3)

The response to this communication is beautiful in its simple trust. God said, *"I am...thy exceeding great reward."* Abraham with the utmost confidence, taking God at His word, asked, If this be so, *"what wilt Thou give me?"* Moreover, he spread out his need before God. He said, as it were, "You have spoken of my seed; You have promised me the land; but I go childless and all my possessions will pass to my servant, Eliezer. You have given me the land and spoken about my seed, but, behold, to me Thou hast given no seed, and a servant is my heir."

THE REWARD OF GRACE (V. 4)

The reply of the Lord came to Abraham and, as ever with God, His gifts exceed our requests. Abraham had asked for a son, and God promised him not only a son but also an inheritance for the seed. Sonship and inheritance are the two great themes of God's reply. The word to Abraham was, *"He that shall come forth out of thine own bowels shall be thine heir,"* and, *"I am the Lord that brought thee out of Ur...to give thee this land to inherit it."* The whole scene illustrates the truth of Romans 8:17, *"If children, then heirs."* Sonship and inheritance, whether for the earthly people of God or the heavenly, are inseparably connected. Our future prospects are connected with our character as sons. If we are sons, we must be heirs. God does not have sons without providing an inheritance for them.

THE RECKONING OF RIGHTEOUSNESS (VV. 5-7)

This beautiful picture illustrates a further truth, that

believers are *"all the sons of God by faith in Christ Jesus"* (Gal. 3:26). Faith existed before, but this is the first time that we read that a man *"believed in the Lord."* We see, too, this faith illustrated in all its simplicity. Abraham was brought from his own circumstances, and all that he was asked to do was to look, and listen, and believe. He was to look away from Sarah, himself, the earth, and everything of nature, and, said the Lord, *"Look now toward heaven."* And as he looked to the stars, he was to listen to what God said, *"So shall thy seed be."* Then we read, *"He believed in the Lord; and He counted it to him for righteousness."*

We know how the Spirit of God has used this picture in Romans 4 to set forth the way the believer in Christ is accounted to be in a righteous condition before God. To us sinners, Christ is presented, and God says as it were, *"look"* and *"listen."* Look toward heaven and fix your eye on Christ in glory, and listen to what God says about Christ. That He has died for all, that God is satisfied with Jesus and His work. Looking to Jesus and listening to what God says, the needy soul believes in Jesus as the One that has died for him. God says of the one that believes, he is reckoned by God to be clear of all his sins and in a righteous condition before God. Further, he is a child of God, and if a child, then an heir.

REMISSION OF SINS (VV. 8-10)

Moreover, Abraham learned that the ground of all blessing must be sacrifice. So we must always remember that the everlasting basis of our blessing is the great sacrifice of Christ. *"Without shedding of blood is no remission."* There may be very different measures of appreciation of the sacrifice of Christ, probably set forth by the different animals that Abraham was told to offer, but sacrifice alone can secure the blessing.

Seeing that all blessing for us depends on the great sacrifice of Christ, it will always be the effort of the enemy to belittle His mighty work. It is ours to contend for the truth and drive away every unclean bird that would deny the sacrifice and trample underfoot the blood of Christ.

Moreover, if the sacrifice is the ground of all blessing, there must be on our side the individual appropriation by faith of the death of Christ. The *"sinking sun,"* the *"deep sleep,"* and the *"horror of great darkness,"* all speak of the exercises of soul in entering into the deep meaning of the Cross. Did not Paul know something of these experiences when, after he saw Christ in the glory, *"he was three days without sight, and neither did eat nor drink"* (Acts 9:9)?

Further, Abraham had to learn that the road to glory is a pathway of suffering. His seed would assuredly enter the Promised Land, but they would first pass through affliction. Thus the four truths of Romans 8:17, that we are sons of God, heirs of Christ, suffering with Christ, and going on to the glory, are exemplified in the story of Abraham, who learned that beyond the furnace of affliction there is the light of the glory to come (see also 1 Pet. 1:2-9).

> *Beyond the storms I'm going, beyond this vale of tears,*
> *Beyond the floods o'erflowing, beyond the changing years;*
> *I'm going to the better land by faith long since possessed:*
> *The glory shines before me, for this is not my rest.*
>
> *The glory shines before me, I know that all is well;*
> *My Father's care is o'er me, His praises I would tell:*
> *The love of Christ constrains me, His blood has washed me white;*
> *Where Jesus is in glory 'tis home, and love, and light.*
>
> *O Lord, we would delight in Thee, and on Thy care depend;*
> *To Thee in every trouble flee, our never failing Friend.*
> *When human cisterns all are dried, Thy fullness is the same;*
> *May we with this be satisfied, and glory in Thy name.*

SEVEN

The Flesh and the Law

Now Sarai Abram's wife bare him no children: and she had an handmaid, an Egyptian, whose name was Hagar. And Sarai said unto Abram, Behold now, the Lord hath restrained me from bearing: I pray thee, go in unto my maid; it may be that I may obtain children by her.

And Abram hearkened to the voice of Sarai. And Sarai Abram's wife took Hagar her maid the Egyptian, after Abram had dwelt ten years in the land of Canaan, and gave her to her husband Abram to be his wife. And he went in unto Hagar, and she conceived: and when she saw that she had conceived, her mistress was despised in her eyes. And Sarai said unto Abram, My wrong be upon thee: I have given my maid into thy bosom; and when she saw that she had conceived, I was despised in her eyes: the Lord judge between me and thee. But Abram said unto Sarai, Behold, thy maid is in thy hand; do to her as it pleaseth thee. And when Sarai dealt hardly with her, she fled from her face.

And the angel of the Lord found her by a fountain of water in the wilderness, by the fountain in the way to Shur. And he said, Hagar, Sarai's maid, whence camest thou? and whither wilt thou go? And she said, I flee from the face of my mistress Sarai. And the angel of the Lord said unto her, Return to thy mistress, and submit thyself under her hands. And the angel of the Lord said unto her, I will multiply thy seed exceedingly, that it shall not be numbered for multitude. And the angel of the Lord said unto her, Behold, thou art with child, and shalt bear a son, and shalt call his name Ishmael; because the Lord hath heard thy affliction. And he will be a wild man; his hand will be against every man, and every man's hand against him; and he shall dwell in the presence of all his brethren.

And she called the name of the Lord that spake unto her, Thou God seest me: for she said, Have I also here looked after Him that seeth me? Wherefore the well was called Beer Lahai Roi; behold, it is between Kadesh and Bered. And Hagar bare Abram a son: and Abram called his son's name, which Hagar bare, Ishmael. And Abram was fourscore and six years old, when Hagar bare Ishmael to Abram. GENESIS 16

In chapter 15, we learned that the blessing has been definitely promised to Abraham in grace on the ground of sacrifice. Thus was set forth the great truth that every blessing, whether for God's earthly or heavenly people, comes to them in grace, yet in perfect righteousness, through the death of Christ.

In this chapter we have the account of Abraham's attempt to secure the promise of the heir through the flesh on the ground of works, that is by his own efforts.

THE TEST

God promised Abraham a son, and Abraham believed God (15:4-6). But his patience was put to the test, for we read, *"Now Sarai, Abram's wife bare him no children."* How then was he to obtain the heir? Under the test, his patience broke down. Instead of waiting for God's time, he attempted to obtain the promised blessing by his own efforts. In the epistle to the Hebrews, Abraham was brought forward as the great example of those who *"through faith and patience inherit the promises"* (Heb. 6:12-15). In his history, as so often with ourselves, we see that on occasions he broke down in the very things of which, in the main, he is a striking example. In chapter 12, as we have seen, his faith failed when put to the test. Here, in chapter 16, his patience breaks down under a fresh test.

THE TEMPTATION

As in the former case, Egypt was at hand to tempt him from the path of faith by relieving him of all the exercises that such a path entails, so the Egyptian maid was at hand to suggest relief from further waiting. Though he himself had been restored, the result of his lapse into Egypt was still manifest. Something of the world had been introduced into his household which, if he acted in the flesh, was ready to be used. How true it is that what a man sows that shall he also reap. Through a careless walk we can easily introduce something of the world into our homes, which in due time will give the flesh an opportunity to manifest itself.

In Galatians 4:21-26, the Apostle Paul refers to this incident and gives us its spiritual meaning. He reminds the Galatian assemblies that Abraham had two sons, one by a bondmaid, the other by the free woman, and that the son of the bondwoman was born after the flesh, but the son of the free woman was by promise.

THE TEACHING

Then he tells us that these things are an allegory setting forth the two covenants—the covenant of law connected with Sinai, which leads to bondage, set forth by Hagar and her son; and the covenant of grace, connected with Jerusalem which is above, leading to liberty, and set forth by Sarah and her son.

THE TENDENCY

The Galatian believers, though truly converted and having the Spirit, were turning back to the law as a rule of life, and were thus, in practice making their blessing depend on their own efforts. To use the language of the allegory, they became the children of Sinai, and developed a character marked by the traits of the flesh. If connected with the liberty of Jerusalem above, which sets forth sovereign grace, they would have shown the character of Christ. Instead of this they were—as the result of putting themselves under law—manifesting a proud, vainglorious spirit which led to envy, so that they were biting and devouring one another, and being drawn into the world (Gal. 4:21; 5:15, 26). The apostle longed that Christ might be formed in them, so that the beautiful character of Christ might shine forth from them (Gal. 4:19).

Turning then to the story of Abraham, we see that the only result of seeking to obtain the heir by his own fleshly efforts was to introduce into his household that which had the character of the flesh, *"That which is born of the flesh is flesh."* Nature can only produce nature. So Abraham's natural efforts only produced the natural man that in due course would persecute the spiritual seed.

THE TRAGEDY

In the meantime, a jarring element was brought into the family. The one who represented the efforts of the flesh despised the one through whom the blessing would come (v. 4). Sarah and Hagar, setting forth what was of the flesh and what was of the Spirit, could not agree, *"for the flesh* [battles] *against the Spirit and the Spirit against the flesh: and these are contrary the one to the other"* (Gal. 5:17). Moreover the man that was brought into his household gravitated toward the world, for he was found in the wilderness of Shur on the borders of Egypt (v. 7). He was, moreover, a hard character who was against every man, and stirred up every man against himself (v. 12).

THE TYPE

The application of these truths to ourselves is plain. We may, like Abraham be true believers, and like the Galatians have the Spirit, and yet in our daily life we may make the law our rule of life. We may thus allow the thought that our being in the favor and grace of God our Father depends on our own good walk and legal efforts. The results will be twofold. First, we develop a hard and self-righteous character that is proud of itself and jealous of others. Secondly, we shall fail to enjoy the liberty wherewith Christ has made us free, and so lack grace and love, entirely failing to produce the fruit of the Spirit that sets forth the character of Christ (Gal. 5:1-6, 22).

THE INTERPRETATION

The interpretation given in Galatians shows that what is set forth in the allegory is not a sinner seeking justification by his works, but rather a believer, who is already justified, seeking holiness of life by his own legal efforts and in his own strength.

It is evident that Christendom has fallen into this Galatian legality. It is not that Christian truths have been entirely given up, but that the legal system set forth by Hagar has been introduced into Christian profession, so that there are many true Christians kept in bondage of soul through seeking to regulate their lives by the law in order to walk well, and thus obtain the favor of God, instead of seeing that right walk flows from the blessed fact that through the death of Christ they are already in the everlasting favor of God, and can only walk rightly in the strength of Christ.

Typically, the story may set forth the history of Israel under the law seeking to obtain the promises by their own works. As a result they found themselves, like Hagar, cast out of their land and wanderers in a wilderness world in which they are contrary to all men and every man against them. Nevertheless the nation is beloved for the father's sake, and hence the providential care of God is never withdrawn from them, even as Hagar found that in the wilderness there was a well and the angel of the Lord, and that God saw all her distress.

> *Child of God, by Christ's salvation,*
> *Rise o'er sin and fear and care—*
> *Joy to find in ev'ry station,*
> *Something still to do or bear;*
> *Think what Spirit dwells within thee!*
> *Think what Father's smiles are thine!*
> *Think that Jesus died to win thee,*
> *Child of God, wilt thou repine?*
>
> *Haste thee on from grace to glory,*
> *Armed by faith and winged by prayer,*
> *Heaven's eternal day's before thee,*
> *God's right hand shall guide thee there;*
> *Soon shall close thine earthly mission,*
> *Soon shall pass thy pilgrim days,*
> *Hope shall change to glad fruition,*
> *Faith to sight, and prayer to praise.* —H. L.

EIGHT

The Almighty God and the Everlasting Covenant

And when Abram was ninety years old and nine, the Lord appeared to Abram, and said unto him, I am the Almighty God; walk before Me, and be thou perfect. And I will make My covenant between Me and thee, and will multiply thee exceedingly. And Abram fell on his face: and God talked with him, saying, As for Me, behold, My covenant is with thee, and thou shalt be a father of many nations. Neither shall thy name any more be called Abram, but thy name shall be Abraham; for a father of many nations have I made thee. And I will make thee exceeding fruitful, and I will make nations of thee, and kings shall come out of thee. And I will establish My covenant between Me and thee and thy seed after thee in their generations for an everlasting covenant, to be a God unto thee, and to thy seed after thee. And I will give unto thee, and to thy seed after thee, the land wherein thou art a stranger, all the land of Canaan, for an everlasting possession; and I will be their God.

And God said unto Abraham, Thou shalt keep My covenant therefore, thou, and thy seed after thee in their generations. This is My covenant, which ye shall keep, between Me and you and thy seed after thee; every man child among you shall be circumcised. And ye shall circumcise the flesh of your foreskin; and it shall be a token of the covenant betwixt Me and you. And he that is eight days old shall be circumcised among you, every man child in your generations, he that is born in the house, or bought with money of any stranger, which is not of thy seed. He that is born in thy house, and he that is bought with thy money, must needs be circumcised: and My covenant shall be in your flesh for an everlasting covenant....

And God said unto Abraham, As for Sarai thy wife, thou shalt not call her name Sarai, but Sarah shall her name be. And I will bless her, and give thee a son also of her: yea, I will bless her, and she shall be a mother of nations; kings of people shall be of her. Then Abraham fell upon his face, and laughed, and said in his heart, Shall a child be born unto him that is an hundred years old? and shall Sarah, that is ninety years old, bear?

And Abraham said unto God, O that Ishmael might live before Thee! And God said, Sarah thy wife shall bear thee a son indeed; and thou shalt call his name Isaac: and I will establish My covenant with him for an everlasting covenant, and with his seed after him. And as for Ishmael, I have heard thee: Behold, I have blessed him, and will make him fruitful, and will multiply him exceedingly; twelve princes shall he beget, and I will make him a great nation. But My covenant will I establish with Isaac, which Sarah shall bear unto thee at this set time in the next year. And He left off talking with him, and God went up from Abraham.

And Abraham took Ishmael his son, and all that were born in his house, and all that were bought with his money, every male among the men of Abraham's house; and circumcised the flesh of their foreskin in the selfsame day, as

God had said unto him...In the selfsame day was Abraham circumcised, and Ishmael his son. And all the men of his house, born in the house, and bought with money of the stranger, were circumcised with him. GENESIS 17

LISTENING TO GOD'S REVELATION OF HIMSELF (VV. 1-2)

In the Epistle to the Hebrews, we read of Abraham that *"after he had patiently endured, he obtained the promises"* (Heb. 6:12-15). The story of Hagar and Ishmael showed that under pressure he failed in patience. That story closed with the statement that *"Abram was fourscore and six years old, when Hagar bare Ishmael to Abram."* Now we read, *"When Abram was ninety years old and nine, the Lord appeared to Abram."* For thirteen years he patiently endured. During these years there is no record of any communications to Abraham. God waited until all hope was gone that the blessing could be obtained by the efforts of the flesh.

Having experienced the futility of his own efforts to obtain the promised heir, and having been kept waiting until he was ninety-nine—thus realized his utter weakness—the Lord appeared to Abraham and revealed Himself as *"the Almighty God."* This, as it has been pointed out, was a great advance on former communications. In chapter 15, we read that God revealed Himself to Abraham as his shield and exceeding great reward. There it was a revelation of what God was for Abraham; here it is a revelation of what God is in Himself.

Connected with this revelation, the Lord said to Abraham, *"Walk before Me, and be thou perfect."* As we saw, Abraham's way had not been altogether perfect. Though he was a man of true faith and patience, in the matter of turning aside to Egypt he had failed in faith; in the matter of Hagar, he had failed in patience. Now, having learned his weakness, he learned that God is Almighty. If God is Almighty, God's purposes and promises would surely come to fruition, however impossible their fulfillment may appear to nature, and sight, and the flesh. Abraham only had to remember that God is Almighty and at once every difficulty would disappear, every obstacle would be surmounted, and in quiet faith and patience he would be enabled to wait for God to act in God's own time. No longer did Abraham expect anything from nature. Everything depended on God from first to last. So God could say, *"I will make My covenant between Me and thee, and will multiply thee exceedingly."* We can say, *"If* God will"; who but the Almighty God can rightly say, "I will"?

FALLING ON HIS FACE BEFORE GOD (V. 3)

The effect of this fresh revelation on Abraham is striking. When the word of the Lord came to Abraham in a vision revealing what God was *for* Abraham, at once Abraham thought of himself, and, in happy confidence spoke to God, spreading out his needs, and stating his difficulties before God. When God personally visited Abraham, revealing who He was in Himself, Abraham fell on his face as a listener, and God spoke to him. He realized his own nothingness in the presence of God's greatness, and at once took the lowly place on his face. The former communications led Abraham to think of himself and his need. This revelation led him to think of God, and formed in him a character that was consistent with the One that met his need: he walked before God.

How beautiful are these practical examples of the blessed intimacies between God and the believer! God so inspired Abraham with the confidence that He was for Him that Abraham could speak with God; then Abraham was brought into the lowly place before God so that God could speak with him.

In our present day we require, and have, these different revelations of God. We need to know all that God is for us in His grace and love; and such knowledge leads to sweet intimacy and communion with God by which we can pour out our needs concerning our difficulties and trials before Him. But we also have the revelation of all that God is in Himself as the Father. This revelation leads to a true sense of our nothingness before Him. At the same time, the heart delighting in its Object is formed into the likeness of the One upon whom we gaze. *"We are changed into the same image from glory to glory."* Thus whether in Abraham's day or in ours, the right appreciation of the revelation of all that the Lord is would lead to be like Him. In this sense, we should walk before the Lord and be perfect.

RECEIVING COMMUNICATIONS FROM GOD (V. 4-8)

We are permitted to hear the blessedness of these communications as God talks with Abraham. First, Abraham was told that the grace of God would flow out to the nations. If God is Almighty, He can overcome every barrier and bless the Gentiles.

Secondly, in connection with the revelation of God as the Almighty, Abraham's name was changed from Abram to Abraham, meaning *"father of a multitude."* Thus God put honor upon His servant.

Thirdly, Abraham was told that he would be exceedingly fruitful. Not only through Abraham would nations be blessed, but through him there would be fruit for God on earth.

Fourthly, while the nations would be blessed, yet Abraham and his seed would be in the closest relationship with God. *"I will establish My covenant,"* said God, *"between Me and thee and thy seed after thee."* And that covenant would be an everlasting covenant by which God covenanted to be the God of Abraham and his seed after him.

Fifthly, God not only made an everlasting covenant, but secured to Abraham and his seed, *"an everlasting possession."*

RESPONSIBILITY TOWARDS GOD (VV. 9-13)

These, then, are some of the blessings of the everlasting covenant that God made with Abraham. The covenant presented God's settled purpose to bless, for seven times in the course of this communication God said, *"I will."* Abraham learned that God looks for an answer to His own grace in the believer's life. Abraham was to walk before God and be perfect.

As Christians, we are not asked—even as Abraham was not asked—to walk well in order to obtain the blessing, but to walk in a way suited to God because *we are* blessed. To thus walk and be perfect before God calls for dependence on God and His almighty power. But this involves the entire refusal of the flesh. To this end circumcision was introduced, as a sign that the flesh is to be mortified if the walk is to be perfect before God. In chapter 15, death was brought in as the ground of justification; here the refusal of the flesh, by that which speaks of death to the flesh, is in order to enjoy holiness in our walk.

If God covenants to bless by His almighty power, there must on our side be no confidence in the flesh or allowance of its activity. For the believer today, circumcision is, *"of the heart, in the spirit, and not in the letter; whose praise is not of men, but of God"* (Rom. 2:29). The refusal of the flesh is not to be merely an outward neglecting of the body of which the world can take account. The refusal of the flesh in all its inward workings is needed. We must reject its self-confidence, self-righteousness, vanity and lusts as that which has been condemned in the cross (Col. 2:11). There is also the solemn reminder that the allowance of the flesh in the believer will lead to governmental judgment, even to cutting off from God's people.

Sarah was blessed with Abraham and was ennobled with a change of name. In the presence of these communications Abraham was filled with joy: for, doubtless, in this passage the laughter speaks of joy, not unbelief.

PLEADING WITH GOD (VV. 18-21)

Abraham pled for Ishmael, and God heard his prayer. Nevertheless, twice over Abraham was reminded that the covenant was established in Abraham's promised son who was to be called Isaac.

From Romans 9:6-9, it would seem that Ishmael pictures the unbelieving mass of Israel. There we read, *"They are not all Israel, which are of Israel: neither, because they are the seed of Abraham, are they all children: but, In Isaac shall thy seed be called."* The unbelieving mass of the nation are children of Abraham according to the flesh; but only the believing remnant are the true seed according to promise. Nevertheless, even the children according to the flesh would be great upon the earth.

KEEPING THE COVENANT WITH GOD (VV. 22-27)

Having finished this great communication, God left off talking with Abraham. The same day Abraham entered into the good of the covenant through the rite of circumcision. He put into practice the word that he heard, and acted consistently with the revelation that God had made of Himself.

O endless joy! how shall my heart
Thy riches all unfold:
Or tell the grace that gave me part,
In bliss no tongue hath told?

Lord! Let me wait for Thee alone:
My life be only this—
To serve Thee here on earth, unknown;
Then share Thy heavenly bliss.

Lord! be it soon! Thou know'st our heart,
In this sad world, no rest
Can find nor wish but where Thou art:
That rest itself possessed!

Soon shall we see Thee as Thou art:
O hope for ever blessed!
Thou'lt call us, in our heavenly part—
The Father's house to rest.

O rest! ineffable, divine,
The rest of God above:
Where Thou forever shalt be mine;
My joy, eternal love!

His counsels, all fulfilled in Thee;
His work of love, complete:
And heavenly hosts shall rest, to see
Earth blest beneath Thy feet. —J. N. D.

NINE

Blessings and Privileges

*And the Lord appeared unto him in the plains of Mamre:
and he sat in the tent door in the heat of the day; and he
lifted up his eyes and looked, and, lo, three men stood by
him: and when he saw them, he ran to meet them from the
tent door, and bowed himself toward the ground, and said,
My Lord, if now I have found favor in Thy sight, pass not
away, I pray Thee, from Thy servant. Let a little water, I
pray You, be fetched, and wash Your feet, and rest
Yourselves under the tree: and I will fetch a morsel of
bread, and comfort Ye Your hearts; after that Ye shall pass
on: for therefore are Ye come to Your servant. And they
said, So do, as thou hast said.*

*And Abraham hastened into the tent unto Sarah, and
said, Make ready quickly three measures of fine meal,
knead it, and make cakes upon the hearth. And Abraham
ran unto the herd, and fetched a calf tender and good, and
gave it unto a young man; and he hasted to dress it. And he
took butter, and milk, and the calf which he had dressed,
and set it before them; and he stood by them under the tree,
and they did eat.*

*And they said unto him, Where is Sarah thy wife? And he
said, Behold, in the tent. And He said, I will certainly*

return unto thee according to the time of life; and, lo, Sarah thy wife shall have a son. And Sarah heard it in the tent door, which was behind him. Now Abraham and Sarah were old and well stricken in age; and it ceased to be with Sarah after the manner of women. Therefore Sarah laughed within herself, saying, After I am waxed old shall I have pleasure, my lord being old also?

And the Lord said unto Abraham, Wherefore did Sarah laugh, saying, Shall I of a surety bear a child, which am old? Is any thing too hard for the Lord? At the time appointed I will return unto thee, according to the time of life, and Sarah shall have a son. Then Sarah denied, saying, I laughed not; for she was afraid. And He said, Nay; but thou didst laugh.

And the men rose up from thence, and looked toward Sodom: and Abraham went with them to bring them on the way. And the Lord said, Shall I hide from Abraham that thing which I do; Seeing that Abraham shall surely become a great and mighty nation, and all the nations of the earth shall be blessed in him? For I know him, that he will command his children and his household after him, and they shall keep the way of the Lord, to do justice and judgment; that the Lord may bring upon Abraham that which He hath spoken of him.

And the Lord said, Because the cry of Sodom and Gomorrah is great, and because their sin is very grievous; I will go down now, and see whether they have done altogether according to the cry of it, which is come unto Me; and if not, I will know. And the men turned their faces from thence, and went toward Sodom: but Abraham stood yet before the Lord. And Abraham drew near, and said, Wilt Thou also destroy the righteous with the wicked? Peradventure there be fifty righteous within the city: wilt Thou also destroy and not spare the place for the fifty

> *righteous that are therein? That be far from Thee to do*
> *after this manner, to slay the righteous with the wicked:*
> *and that the righteous should be as the wicked, that be far*
> *from Thee: shall not the Judge of all the earth do right?*
> *And the Lord said, If I find in Sodom fifty righteous within*
> *the city, then I will spare all the place for their sakes...forty*
> *and five...forty...thirty...twenty...ten...And He said, I will*
> *not destroy it for ten's sake. And the Lord went His way, as*
> *soon as He had left communing with Abraham: and*
> *Abraham returned unto his place.* GENESIS 18

In chapter 17 we learned how God revealed Himself to Abraham as the Almighty—the One who can and will fulfill His promises of blessing in spite of every difficulty. In the light of this revelation, Abraham was to walk before God and be perfect, having no confidence in the flesh.

In chapter 18 we are permitted to see the blessings and privileges of one whose walk is consistent with the revelation of God as the Almighty. The chapter unfolds four great privileges that such a person can enjoy. First he had the personal manifestation of the Lord to him (vv. 1-8). Secondly, he had the assurance of the coming blessing through the promised heir (vv. 9-15). Thirdly, he was treated as a friend to whom God confided what He was about to do (vv. 16-21). Fourthly, in confidence and nearness to God, he could intercede on behalf of others (vv. 22-33).

DIVINE VISITATION (VV. 1-7)

The first great privilege that the believer enjoys, who walks before God in the light of the revelation that God has given of Himself, and who has no confidence in the flesh, is the personal manifestation of the Lord.

The chapter opens with Abraham sitting at his tent door. As a stranger with his tent, he was at rest outside the strife of this world. Is there not a danger in our day of believers being distracted and excited by over-occupation with the events taking place in the world? Would that we knew more of the rest of spirit that is the outcome of answering to the call of God and taking the outside place in confidence in God and having no confidence in the flesh! To such people God comes, as in the case of Abraham, to commune in the most intimate way.

The manner of His coming is striking. Abraham looked up and saw that *"three men stood by him."* As the story develops, we learn that two were angels who in due course appeared as such in the gate of Sodom (19:1). The other, we know, was none less than the Lord Himself appearing in human form, a foreshadowing of the time when the Son of God would become Incarnate and dwell among the children of men.

DIVINE MINISTRY (VV. 6-8)

Apparently there was no outward token by which Abraham or others could have discerned the presence of Jehovah. All that the world would have seen were three men at his tent door. Abraham, with the spiritual discernment of a man of faith walking in nearness to God, distinguished the Lord from the two angels, and in reverence bowed himself to the ground and addressed Him personally, for he said, *"Lord, if now I have found favor in Thy sight, pass not away, I pray Thee, from Thy servant."* He asked to be allowed to wash their feet (the first occurrence in Scripture), and invited them to rest under the shadow of the tree while he prepared refreshment before them.

Abraham was permitted to do as he had said. A meal was set before them, *"and he stood by them under the tree, and they did eat."* Today, if we are walking in the deeper knowledge of God revealed as Father, is it not possible for believers to enjoy this sweet and intimate fellowship with the divine Persons? Not in the particular way in which the Lord appeared to Abraham, but by the Spirit who has come from the Father, we can be led into the most blessed communion. Little we may know of it, but, nonetheless it can be known.

On that last night in the Upper Room, the Lord intimated that when He left the disciples it would still be possible for them to enjoy—in the power of the Spirit—an intimacy far deeper than any they had known while the Lord was present with them. Having spoken of the Spirit that the Father would send, He said, *"At that day,"* the day in which we live, *"he that hath My commandments, and keepeth them, he it is that loveth Me: and he that loveth Me shall be loved of My Father, and I will love him, and will manifest Myself to him"* and then adds, *"If a man love Me, he will keep My words: and My Father will love him and We will come unto Him, and make Our abode with him"* (Jn. 14:16-25).

Here, too, for the first time we have the mention of feet washing in Scripture. As elsewhere, the thought of feet washing is to refresh the one whose feet are washed. Abraham had the high privilege of washing the feet of the One who, in the years to come, would become flesh and, in the greatness of the love that delighted to serve others would, in His condescending grace, wash His poor disciples' feet.

Divine Communication (vv. 9-15)

The Lord took this occasion, this moment of holy intimacy, to confirm the faith of Abraham by assuring him of the coming birth of his son. This concerned Sarah, so the Lord asked, *"Where is Sarah thy wife?"* Then the Lord said, *"I will certainly return unto thee at this time of the year; and behold, Sarah thy wife shall have a son"* (New

TRANS.). For any but a divine Person to have spoken thus would have been mere presumption. We cannot count on one day. God can say, *"I will certainly return."* Thus the faith of Abraham was confirmed by the assurance of the Lord's own words. And still the Lord delights to assure our trembling hearts with the certain word of the One who can say, "I will." *"I will come again, and receive you unto Myself." "I will not leave you comfortless: I will come to you"* (Jn. 14:3, 18).

Abraham heard this great promise with the full realization of the glory of the One who spoke, and therefore expressed no astonishment, raised no difficulties, and expressed no doubt. In marked contrast, Sarah's faith and discernment was not equal to her husband's. She heard what was said, but had little realization of the glory of the Speaker. She doubted what was said because of what she found in herself. She was old and her body worn out, therefore she argued that what the Lord had said could not come true, and in her heart she laughed in unbelief at the very suggestion of having a son. She was rebuked for her unbelief and Abraham was reminded that, however impossible the fulfillment of the promise on the ground of nature, there is nothing too hard for the Lord.

Charged with her unbelief, Sarah was ashamed to acknowledge the truth. As so often is the case, fear of consequences leads to lying and deceit. She *"denied, saying, I laughed not."* It may have been true that she did not laugh aloud; but she laughed in her heart and had to learn that she was in the presence of One who could see behind tent doors and read the heart.

DIVINE PROPHECY (VV. 16-21)

In the years to come, God spoke through the prophet Isaiah of Abraham as *"My friend"* (Isa. 41:8). In this scene we see God treating Abraham as a friend. Truly, as has often been said, we speak to a servant about things that concern his work; to a friend we speak of that which we may be about to do, though it may not be his direct concern. Abraham was treated as a friend, for God said, *"Shall I hide from Abraham that thing which I do?"* The reason that God treated him as a friend was blessed, for, the Lord said, *"I know him, that he will command his children and his household after him, and they shall keep the way of the Lord, to do justice and judgment."* The one that the Lord treated as a friend was not only one that believed in the Lord, but also led his household in the fear of the Lord.

To us the word of the Lord is, *"Ye are My friends, if ye do whatsoever I command you";* and He adds, *"Henceforth I call you not servants; for the servant knoweth not what his Lord doeth: but I have called you friends; for all things that I have heard of My Father I have made known unto you"* (Jn. 15:14, 15).

Treating Abraham as a friend, the Lord told him of the judgment that He was about to bring upon the cities of the plain. But let us remember that these communications come to the man who, as we have seen, lived apart from the world, had renounced the world, and gained the victory over the world. Unless we escape the corruptions of the world, we shall be saying with the mere professor, *"Where is the promise of His coming?"* The Apostle Peter warns us not to be in ignorance of the solemn fact that the day of the Lord will come as a thief in the night, bringing judgment on an ungodly world.

Already we have learned that *"the men of Sodom were wicked and sinners before the Lord exceedingly"* (13:13). We learn that their sin cried out to the Lord for judgment, for it was *"very grievous."* God waited and bore long with the wickedness of men, but He was not indifferent to sin. It cried out to Him until at last it was ripe for judgment. But, even so, the Lord was slow to judge. First we read of the two angels, that they *"rose up from thence, and looked toward Sodom"* (v. 16); then they *"went toward Sodom"* (v. 22); finally, we read, *"there came two angels to Sodom at even"* (19:1).

INTERCESSION (VV. 22-33)

Two angels had passed on to execute the judgment of the Lord on the doomed cities. Abraham was left alone, standing before the Lord. At once he took the place of the intercessor. He interceded on the ground that it was impossible to destroy the righteous with the wicked. Therefore he pled with God to spare the city if there were found fifty righteous men in it. Then he pled for it to be saved if there were forty-five righteous men; then he comes down to forty, thirty, twenty, and at last he pled if there were only ten men. Each time God, in His grace, granted his request; until, at last, Abraham's faith drew upon that grace of God that, where sin abounds, grace does much more abound.

At a later date God said to Jeremiah of the doomed city of Jerusalem, *"If ye can find a man, if there be any that executeth judgment, that seeketh the truth; and I will pardon it"* (Jer. 5:1). We now know that such a Man has been found: Christ is the *"One mediator between God and men, the Man Christ Jesus who gave Himself a ransom for all."* Through this Man we are bidden to intercede for all men (1 Tim. 2:1-6).

> *What is the garish world to me—*
> *Its tinsel and its joys?*
> *Thy glory and Thy grace I see,*
> *My soul is satisfied with Thee,*
> *And earth no more annoys.*

TEN

Friendship with the World

And there came two angels to Sodom at even; and Lot sat in the gate of Sodom: and Lot seeing them rose up to meet them; and he bowed himself with his face toward the ground; and he said, Behold now, my lords, turn in, I pray you, into your servant's house, and tarry all night, and wash your feet, and ye shall rise up early, and go on your ways. And they said, Nay; but we will abide in the street all night. And he pressed upon them greatly; and they turned in unto him, and entered into his house; and he made them a feast, and did bake unleavened bread, and they did eat.

But before they lay down, the men of the city, even the men of Sodom, compassed the house round, both old and young, all the people from every quarter: and they called unto Lot, and said unto him, Where are the men which came in to thee this night? bring them out unto us, that we may know them. And Lot went out at the door unto them, and shut the door after him, And said, I pray you, brethren, do not so wickedly. Behold now, I have two daughters which have not known man; let me, I pray you, bring them out unto you, and do ye to them as is good in your eyes: only unto these men do nothing; for therefore came they under the shadow of my roof. And they said, Stand back.

And they said again, This one fellow came in to sojourn, and he will needs be a judge: now will we deal worse with thee, than with them. And they pressed sore upon the man, even Lot, and came near to break the door. But the men put forth their hand, and pulled Lot into the house to them, and shut to the door. And they smote the men that were at the door of the house with blindness, both small and great: so that they wearied themselves to find the door.

And the men said unto Lot, Hast thou here any besides? son in law, and thy sons, and thy daughters, and whatsoever thou hast in the city, bring them out of this place: for we will destroy this place, because the cry of them is waxen great before the face of the Lord; and the Lord hath sent us to destroy it. And Lot went out, and spake unto his sons in law, which married his daughters, and said, Up, get you out of this place; for the Lord will destroy this city. But he seemed as one that mocked unto his sons in law.

And when the morning arose, then the angels hastened Lot, saying, Arise, take thy wife, and thy two daughters, which are here; lest thou be consumed in the iniquity of the city. And while he lingered, the men laid hold upon his hand, and upon the hand of his wife, and upon the hand of his two daughters; the Lord being merciful unto him: and they brought him forth, and set him without the city.

And it came to pass, when they had brought them forth abroad, that he said, Escape for thy life; look not behind thee, neither stay thou in all the plain; escape to the mountain, lest thou be consumed. And Lot said unto them, Oh, not so, my Lord: Behold now, thy servant hath found grace in thy sight, and thou hast magnified thy mercy, which thou hast showed unto me in saving my life; and I cannot escape to the mountain, lest some evil take me, and I die: Behold now, this city is near to flee unto, and it is a little one: Oh, let me escape thither, (is it not a little one?) and my soul shall live. And he said unto him, See, I have accepted thee concerning this thing also, that I will not overthrow this city, for the which thou hast spoken. Haste thee, escape thither; for I cannot do anything till thou be come thither. Therefore the name of the city was called Zoar.

The sun was risen upon the earth when Lot entered into Zoar. Then the Lord rained upon Sodom and upon Gomorrah brimstone and fire from the Lord out of heaven; and He overthrew those cities, and all the plain, and all the inhabitants of the cities, and that which grew upon the ground. But his wife looked back from behind him, and she became a pillar of salt.

And Abraham got up early in the morning to the place where he stood before the Lord: and he looked toward Sodom and Gomorrah, and toward all the land of the plain, and beheld, and, lo, the smoke of the country went up as the smoke of a furnace. And it came to pass, when God destroyed the cities of the plain, that God remembered Abraham, and sent Lot out of the midst of the overthrow, when He overthrew the cities in the which Lot dwelt.

And Lot went up out of Zoar, and dwelt in the mountain, and his two daughters with him; for he feared to dwell in Zoar: and he dwelt in a cave, he and his two daughters. And the firstborn said unto the younger, Our father is old, and there is not a man in the earth to come in unto us after the manner of all the earth: Come, let us make our father drink wine, and we will lie with him, that we may preserve seed of our father. And they made their father drink wine that night: and the firstborn went in, and lay with her father; and he perceived not when she lay down, nor when she arose. And it came to pass on the morrow, that the firstborn said unto the younger, Behold, I lay yesternight with my father: let us make him drink wine this night also; and go thou in, and lie with him, that we may preserve seed of

our father. And they made their father drink wine that night
also: and the younger arose, and lay with him; and he per-
ceived not when she lay down, nor when she arose. Thus
were both the daughters of Lot with child by their father.
And the firstborn bare a son, and called his name Moab:
the same is the father of the Moabites unto this day. And
the younger, she also bare a son, and called his name
Benammi: the same is the father of the children of Ammon
unto this day.   GENESIS 19

In chapter 18 we saw the blessings of a believer whose
walk is consistent with the revelation of God as the
Almighty. In chapter 19 there comes before us the sorrows
of a believer who has given up the separate path, and walks
in association with a judgment-doomed world. We shall
see, indeed, that he is saved, but so as by fire (1 Cor. 3:15),
and passes out of the story under a cloud, leaving behind
him the memory of a life of shame.

A STRIKING CONTRAST

The opening verses of these two chapters evidently set
Abraham and Lot in striking contrast. In chapter 18:1,
Abraham comes before us as sitting in his tent door. In
chapter 19:1, Lot is seen sitting *"in the gate of Sodom."*
One believer was outside the world in his true pilgrim character, with his tent; the other was not only in the world, he
was actually taking part in its administration. He sat in the
gate—the place of judgment.

THE END OF A DOWNWARD PATH

Once Lot was in the outside place, but there only as a
follower of others. A little trouble arose and at once he
gave up the path of faith and separation, chose the
well-watered plain, and *"pitched his tent toward Sodom"*

(13:12). Next we learn that he *"dwelt in Sodom"* (14:12). At last, we read, *"Lot sat in the gate of Sodom."*

But the city in which Lot had an honored place as a magistrate, was a judgment-doomed city, and the time had come when the city was ripe for judgment. From the Lord's own words, in Luke 17, we know that this solemn scene is a foreshadowing of the judgment about to fall on this present evil world. There we read, *"As it was in the days of Lot...thus shall it be in the day when the Son of Man is revealed"* (Lk. 17:28-32).

We are living in the days just before the Son of Man is about to be revealed, and we are warned by the Lord Himself that in these days we shall find a terrible condition similar to that which existed in the days of Lot. This makes this chapter of immense practical importance, as presenting the true character of the world around us, and, above all, as setting forth conditions so hateful to God that at length He has to intervene in judgment.

THE BREAKDOWN OF TESTIMONY

What then were the conditions in Sodom that brought down the judgment of God? Two things characterized the city. First, the men of Sodom were *"wicked and sinners before the Lord exceedingly"* (13:13). Secondly, a true believer was holding a place of honor in the city, associated with sinners in seeking to judge and maintain order in the world. It was a city characterized by the association of sinners before the Lord with believers in the Lord. It is this condition, so hateful to God, that marks the world of today, and that will very soon bring the present period of grace to a close. It was not simply the wickedness of the world that ends the day of grace. The wickedness of the world may show itself in different forms at different times, but it cannot be greater today than when it perpetrated the crowning sin of crucifying the Lord of glory. It is rather the break-down of the Christian profession whereby even true believers are found in the world, not as witnesses to the grace of God, but in closest association with the world, that God will not tolerate and that makes the judgment so imminent. When those who were left to be a witness to the grace of God settle down in the world and cease to be any witness for God, the end is not far off.

THE MESSAGE OF WARNING

We have the warning challenge of the apostle in clear and unmistakable words, *"Be ye not unequally yoked together with unbelievers: for what fellowship hath righteousness with unrighteousness? and what communion hath light with darkness? And what concord hath Christ with Belial? or what part hath he that believeth with an infidel?"* (2 Cor. 6:14-15).

In spite of these plain words, what do we see on every hand today? Not only a world filled with violence and corruption—this has ever been, although men wax worse and worse—but, on every hand we see true believers in flagrant disregard of the Word of God, associated with unbelievers and those who mock at divine things. It has been truly said, "Evangelical leaders even, can now take their places openly on public platforms with Unitarians and skeptics of almost every grade; and societies, secret or public, can link together all possible beliefs in the most hearty fellowship. It is this that marks the time as so near the limit of divine long-suffering, that the very people who are orthodox as to Christ can nevertheless be so easily content to leave Him aside on any utilitarian plea by which they may have fellowship with His rejectors."

When those who profess to be ministers of Christianity cease to be witnesses for Christ and, sinking down to the level of the world, become themselves the leaders in all worldliness, then indeed the salt has lost its savor and the Christian profession, having become nauseous to Christ, will be spued out of His mouth and the judgment will fall upon the world.

Surely, then, the destruction of Sodom should speak to every conscience and lead us to take heed to that word which says, *"Come out of her, My people, that ye be not partakers of her sins, and that ye receive not of her plagues"* (Rev. 18:4).

THE MINISTRY OF ANGELS

There are, moreover, other lessons for us to learn from this solemn scene. In the preceding chapter, the Lord appeared to Abraham accompanied by two angels. Here it was only the angels that came to Lot (although the Lord was there unseen, 18:21). Abraham, in the outside place with his tent, enjoyed sweet communion with the Lord. Lot, sitting in the gate of Sodom, would have no visits from the Lord. His soul may have been vexed with the filthy conversation and unlawful deeds of the wicked, but he would enjoy no communion with the Lord.

Furthermore, while the Lord came to Abraham in the full light of day, the two angels came to Sodom *"at even."* They came, not to give a public witness to Sodom, but, as it were, in the secrecy of the evening gloom to pull a falling saint out of the fire of judgment (18:1; 19:1).

We may gather from Scripture that the service of angels has a twofold character. On the one hand they are the executors of judgment; on the other hand they are *"ministering spirits sent forth to minister for them who shall be heirs of salvation"* (Ps. 104:4; Heb. 1:14). We see them in this twofold service at Sodom. In judgment they came to destroy the city; providentially, they were there to rescue a true believer from a false position! Good to know that, in our day, though judgment is about to fall on Christendom, every true believer will be saved from judgment, even though with many it may be like Lot, their works destroyed but they themselves saved yet so *"as through the fire"* (1 Cor. 3:15, NEW TRANS.).

LOT'S INCONSISTENCY

Further we see that Lot, being a true believer, recognized the heavenly visitors, treated them with due reverence, sought to honor them, and shelter them from the insults of the men of the world. Alas! he found that he had no power to restrain their wickedness. In his extremity he was even prepared to sink to the vile expedient of abandoning his two daughters to their lust in order to quell the disturbance. His efforts only aroused the anger of the men of Sodom. They told him to *"stand back."* They argued that this man, who came into their midst as an alien, now took upon himself to act as their judge. With these threatening words they pressed hard on Lot who was only saved from the violence of the mob by the providential action of the angels.

LOT'S FAILURE

The angels' directions to Lot to warn his relatives that the Lord was about to destroy the city brought to light the solemn fact that the believer in a false position has no power in testimony. Lot *"went out and spake unto his sons in law,"* warning them of the coming judgment. *"But he seemed as one that mocked."* It was indeed a witness to the truth, but it condemned him. Had he not professed to be a righteous man? And yet he had been so attracted to Sodom that he had chosen to dwell there, even taking a leading part in its affairs. Did he then really believe that the Lord was about to destroy the city? His whole life was a flat contradiction to his testimony. Little wonder that he seemed as one that mocked to the men of Sodom.

Nor is it otherwise today. Can we wonder that the world pays little heed to any warnings uttered by the professed ministers of religion who themselves are leaders in worldliness?

LOT'S HESITATION

Even while warning others, Lot was loath to leave Sodom; for when urged to hurry from the doomed city, we read *"he lingered."* Nevertheless, the mercy of the Lord *"brought him forth and set him without the city."* His wife and two daughters were brought out with him but all his possessions were left behind. He was saved so as through the fire.

Delivered by the mercy of God, he was told to *"escape to the mountain."* He admitted the mercy that had saved him, but he had little faith in the preserving care of the One that directed him to the mountain. Moved by fear and unbelief, he pled that the little city of Zoar would be spared for a place of refuge. His prayer was granted, and as the sun rose Lot enters Zoar.

How solemn are these words, *"The sun was risen."* It speaks of a cloudless day with no sign of the coming judgment. As the Lord tells us of the men of Sodom, *"they did eat, they drank, they bought, they sold, they planted, they builded."* All went on as usual, *"But the same day that Lot went out of Sodom it rained fire and brimstone from heaven and destroyed them all."* The Lord adds the solemn words, *"Even thus shall it be in the day when the Son of Man is revealed"* (Lk. 17:28-30). So, at a later day, the Apostle could write *"that the day of the Lord so cometh as a thief in the night. For when they shall say, Peace and safety; then sudden destruction cometh upon them, as travail upon a woman with child; and they shall not escape"* (1 Thess. 5:2-3).

LOT'S WIFE

Lot's wife looked back. Lot personally was a righteous man, though caught in the toils of the world. His wife was a mere professor who, though she left the city, had her heart still there. She looked back to the place of her affections and became an everlasting warning to professors who, in a moment of fear, may separate from the world but have never known the call of the Lord. How solemn are the Lord's own words, *"Remember Lot's wife"* (Lk. 17:32).

In contrast to Lot, saved through fire, and his wife who looked back, we have a glimpse of the separate man who looked beyond to the city which has foundations. Abraham was in *"the place where he stood before the Lord."* He saw from afar the destruction of the cities of the plain. Then we learn what is so highly instructive, that if Lot was saved from the overthrow of the cities it was because *"God remembered Abraham."* Lot, as he sat in the gate of Sodom, might have said, *"What good is Abraham to the world, dwelling apart in his tent?"* Yet it was of Abraham, in the separate path, that God said, *"Thou shalt be a blessing,"* So it came to pass; for if Lot was saved, it was because God remembered Abraham.

LOT'S FEAR

Though saved from the doom of Sodom, poor Lot was still the victim of fear. The very city of his choice he feared to dwell in, so he fell back on the mountain to which he had been told to flee. But even so, he went to the mountain driven by fear of men rather than led by faith in God. There he became involved in the infamy of his daughters to pass from the history with no record of his end, leaving behind a posterity that became the constant enemy of God's people.

How solemn and searching to all our hearts is this history of a believer who, though once in the path of separation from the world, gave it up to sink into association with the world. There he found that he could have no communion with God; no power to restrain the evil of the world; no power to witness to the truth; and no confidence in the preserving care of God. Finally he passed from the scene under the dark shadow of great shame. Well indeed, if the story leads us to feel our own weakness, and casts us on the One who is able to keep us from falling and present us faultless before the presence of His glory with exceeding joy (Jude 1:24). Better still if we look about us to find some poor brother Lot and heed the verse before: *"And others save with fear, pulling them out of the fire; hating even the garment spotted by the flesh"* (Jude 1:23).

Farewell to this world's fleeting joys,
Our home is not below;
There was no home for Jesus here,
And 'tis to Him we go.

Up to our Father's house we go,
To that sweet home of love:
Many the mansions that are found
Where Jesus dwells above.

And He who left that home above,
To be a sufferer here,
Has left this world again for us
A mansion to prepare.

His errand to the earth was love,
To wretches such as we!
To pluck us from the jaws of death,
Nailed to th' accursed tree.

The accursed tree was the reward
Which this sad world did give
To Him who gave His precious life
That this lost world might live.

And has this world a charm for us,
Where Jesus suffered thus?
No! we have died to all its charms
Through Jesus' wondrous cross.

Farewell, farewell, poor faithless world,
With all your boasted store;
We'd not have joy where He had woe—
Be rich where He was poor.

—F. C. JENNINGS

ELEVEN

The Works of the Flesh

And Abraham journeyed from thence toward the south country, and dwelled between Kadesh and Shur, and sojourned in Gerar. And Abraham said of Sarah his wife, She is my sister: and Abimelech king of Gerar sent, and took Sarah. But God came to Abimelech in a dream by night, and said to him, Behold, thou art but a dead man, for the woman which thou hast taken; for she is a man's wife. But Abimelech had not come near her: and he said, Lord, wilt thou slay also a righteous nation? Said he not unto me, She is my sister? and she, even she herself said, He is my brother: in the integrity of my heart and innocency of my hands have I done this.

And God said unto him in a dream, Yea, I know that thou didst this in the integrity of thy heart; for I also withheld thee from sinning against Me: therefore suffered I thee not to touch her. Now therefore restore the man his wife; for he is a prophet, and he shall pray for thee, and thou shalt live: and if thou restore her not, know thou that thou shalt surely die, thou, and all that are thine.

Therefore Abimelech rose early in the morning, and called all his servants, and told all these things in their ears: and the men were sore afraid. Then Abimelech called Abraham, and said unto him, What hast thou done unto us?

and what have I offended thee, that thou hast brought on me and on my kingdom a great sin? Thou hast done deeds unto me that ought not to be done. And Abimelech said unto Abraham, What sawest thou, that thou hast done this thing? And Abraham said, Because I thought, Surely the fear of God is not in this place; and they will slay me for my wife's sake. And yet indeed she is my sister; she is the daughter of my father, but not the daughter of my mother; and she became my wife. And it came to pass, when God caused me to wander from my father's house, that I said unto her, This is thy kindness which thou shalt show unto me; at every place whither we shall come, say of me, He is my brother.

And Abimelech took sheep, and oxen, and menservants, and womenservants, and gave them unto Abraham, and restored him Sarah his wife. And Abimelech said, Behold, my land is before thee: dwell where it pleaseth thee. And unto Sarah he said, Behold, I have given thy brother a thousand pieces of silver: behold, he is to thee a covering of the eyes, unto all that are with thee, and with all other: thus she was reproved. So Abraham prayed unto God: and God healed Abimelech, and his wife, and his maidservants; and they bare children. For the Lord had fast closed up all the wombs of the house of Abimelech, because of Sarah Abraham's wife.   GENESIS 20

In chapter 19 we saw Abraham in the high places *"where he stood before the Lord,"* outside the world and preserved from the hour of trial that came on those that dwelt on the earth.

AN OLD REPEATED SIN

In chapter 20 Abraham once again journeyed toward the south country, dwelling on the border of Egypt. In this doubtful position he again acted in a way that brought him under rebuke from the man of the world.

Abraham failed in the same way that he had done some twenty years before, though the circumstances were different. Then, under the stress of famine, he had turned aside from the land and slipped into Egypt. Here, without any such trying circumstances, but simply from the fear of man, he denied the one through whom God had definitely assured him the promised heir would come (18:10). In one case he gave up the testimony of the inheritance; in the other he beclouded the testimony to the heir. As then, so now, behind every failure of the people of God, the enemy is attacking some great truth connected with their calling. Today he is especially attacking the truth concerning the true relationship of the Church to her Head in heaven.

The fact that after so many years Abraham should fail in the same way only aggravated the offense. For it was no mere novice in the path of faith, but one who had walked long in the outside place of separation from the world who broke down. Yet it is true to our natures that there are weak spots in each personality which first show signs of strain when we are brought under pressure. How we need to be honest with the Lord about these areas and seek, as Paul did, to find that His *"grace is sufficient for thee"* for His strength is made perfect in our weakness (2 Cor. 12:9).

Another great lesson that we can learn from this sad episode is that the flesh in God's people never changes. This is a solemn truth that we are slow to realize, but that we all have to learn, at times through bitter experience. There is grace to deliver us from the power of the flesh, and to keep us from its evil; but the evil flesh from which we are kept never changes. The flesh may tend to show itself in different forms in different individuals; but whatever form its evil may take, that is the form of evil it will retain from the beginning of our history to the end.

This twice repeated failure on the part of this man of God is surely recounted, not to discourage us or turn us back on our weakness, but rather to cast us on the true source of all confidence and strength. One has truly said, it is only when we have learned that we are "unable to do without God for a moment that we find that He is for us moment by moment." But it is easy to say that we cannot do without God; it is a harder thing to learn experimentally, perhaps by repeated failure, that we are dependent on God moment by moment.

With the fear of man in him, Abraham lost faith in God. Failing in faith, he fell back on his own resources and acted in the duplicity of the flesh. He said of Sarah, his wife, *"She is my sister."* He told the truth to hide the truth, and again exposed his wife to shame to preserve his own life.

A GOD EVER FAITHFUL

Nevertheless, however great their failure, God does not give up His people. He will never cast away His pearls because of some grit that attaches to them. He will deal with all in us that is contrary to Himself—it may be at painful cost to us—in order to make us partakers of His holiness. And not only does God deal with us after the fact, He acts preemptively for His poor failing people. So in this case God intervened in a marked way to preserve Sarah from the shame to which Abraham's duplicity had exposed her. Abimelech was kept from wronging Abraham and Sarah, and was even warned that Abraham was a prophet. He was told in no uncertain terms that unless Sarah was at once restored to Abraham, death would surely come to his household. Further, Abimelech was informed in the dream that the very man who had so wronged him was one who was in such a position of nearness to God that he could pray for him. In spite of his failure, he was a prophet and an intercessor with God: and God did not deny these high privileges because of his failures.

A REBUKE JUSTIFIED

Nevertheless, the privileges of being a prophet and an intercessor only increased the evil of his duplicity. This the world was not slow to appreciate; for at once Abimelech called Abraham, and challenged him as to what he had done. In plain language Abimelech said, *"Thou hast done deeds unto me that ought not to be done."* Not only had Abraham failed in faith in God, not only had he wronged his wife, he had wronged the man of the world. Abraham had sunk not only beneath the height of his calling but beneath the conduct of a decent man of the world.

Further, Abimelech challenged Abraham as to what led him to do this thing. Abraham answered, *"I thought, surely the fear of God is not in this place; and they will kill me for my wife's sake."* How low this man of God had fallen. Carried away by his own thoughts, thinking only of himself and his safety, he acted with a duplicity that clearly showed that at that moment he himself had not the fear of God before him, however much he may charge others with the lack of it.

A LAME EXCUSE

As so often is the case when a believer fails there is the effort to palliate the failure, instead of honest confession, "I have sinned." No three words in human language are so hard for either a sinner or a saint to utter as these words. So Abraham sought to excuse his duplicity by explaining that it was quite true that Sarah was his sister, even though he had held back the truth that she was also his wife. It has been well stated: "When the devil encourages a half-truth,

he wants people to believe the wrong half."

An Unjudged Root of Unbelief

Moreover, it came out that this failure had an unjudged root of unbelief far back in his history. In a false position, he lowered the testimony of God to the apprehension of the world, by saying, *"When God caused me to wander from my father's house."* He did not say, *"When God called me to a heavenly country and a city which has foundations,"* but he gave the impression that, like any mere prodigal, God had caused him to wander from his father's house. In these circumstances he and his wife had entered into a compact of unbelieving duplicity.

A Conduct Unbecoming

In spite of Abraham's failure, Abimelech, man of the world though he was, acted in a righteous and even liberal way that was in striking contrast to Abraham's conduct. In the day of power and victory over the enemy, Abraham refused to take *"from a thread even to a shoe latchet"* from the king of Sodom. In the day of weakness and unbelief, he would accept sheep, oxen, menservants, womenservants, and a thousand pieces of silver from the king of Gerar.

Nevertheless, though giving gifts to Abraham, Abimelech did not hesitate to reprove his wife in terms of contempt, for he said, *"Behold, I have given thy brother a thousand pieces of silver: behold, he is to thee a covering of the eyes."* Had she been rightly veiled, as Abraham's wife, she never would have been seen by Abimelech or taken into his house. The veil spoke of the women being exclusively for the one to whom she belonged.

As believers, if it were seen that we were exclusively for Christ, the world would not wish to have us in its company. Paul could say, *"For to me to live is Christ."* As a result the world was crucified to him, and he was crucified to the world. Failing to maintain this single-hearted devotedness to Christ, we shall like Sarah lose the respect of the world and come under its just reproof.

The root of their failure being exposed, Abraham once again resumed his true place in reference to the world as an intercessor (vv. 17-18).

God moves in a mysterious way,
His wonders to perform;
He plants His footsteps in the sea,
And rides upon the storm.

Deep in unfathomable mines,
Of never-failing skill,
He treasures up His bright designs,
And works His sovereign will.

Ye fearful saints, fresh courage take,
The clouds ye so much dread
Are big with mercy, and will break
In blessings on your head.

Judge not the Lord by feeble sense,
But trust Him for His grace:
Behind a frowning providence
He hides a smiling face.

His purposes will ripen fast,
Unfolding every hour;
The bud may have a bitter taste,
But sweet will be the flower.

Blind unbelief is sure to err,
And scan His work in vain;
God is His own interpreter,
And He will make it plain. —W. COWPER

TWELVE

The Birth of the Heir

And the Lord visited Sarah as He had said, and the Lord did unto Sarah as He had spoken. For Sarah conceived, and bare Abraham a son in his old age, at the set time of which God had spoken to him. And Abraham called the name of his son that was born unto him, whom Sarah bare to him, Isaac. And Abraham circumcised his son Isaac being eight days old, as God had commanded him. And Abraham was an hundred years old, when his son Isaac was born unto him. And Sarah said, God hath made me to laugh, so that all that hear will laugh with me. And she said, Who would have said unto Abraham, that Sarah should have given children suck? for I have born him a son in his old age.

And the child grew, and was weaned: and Abraham made a great feast the same day that Isaac was weaned. And Sarah saw the son of Hagar the Egyptian, which she had born unto Abraham, mocking. Wherefore she said unto Abraham, Cast out this bondwoman and her son: for the son of this bondwoman shall not be heir with my son, even with Isaac. And the thing was very grievous in Abraham's sight because of his son. And God said unto Abraham, Let it not be grievous in thy sight because of the lad, and because of thy bondwoman; in all that Sarah hath said unto thee, hearken unto her voice; for in Isaac shall thy seed be called. And also of the son of the bondwoman will I make a nation, because he is thy seed.

And Abraham rose up early in the morning, and took bread, and a bottle of water, and gave it unto Hagar, putting it on her shoulder, and the child, and sent her away: and she departed, and wandered in the wilderness of Beersheba. And the water was spent in the bottle, and she cast the child under one of the shrubs. And she went, and sat her down over against him a good way off, as it were a bowshot: for she said, Let me not see the death of the child.

And she sat over against him, and lift up her voice, and wept. And God heard the voice of the lad; and the angel of God called to Hagar out of heaven, and said unto her, What aileth thee, Hagar? fear not; for God hath heard the voice of the lad where he is. Arise, lift up the lad, and hold him in thine hand; for I will make him a great nation. And God opened her eyes, and she saw a well of water; and she went, and filled the bottle with water, and gave the lad drink. And God was with the lad; and he grew, and dwelt in the wilderness, and became an archer. And he dwelt in the wilderness of Paran: and his mother took him a wife out of the land of Egypt.

And it came to pass at that time, that Abimelech and Phichol the chief captain of his host spake unto Abraham, saying, God is with thee in all that thou doest: now therefore swear unto me here by God that thou wilt not deal falsely with me, nor with my son, nor with my son's son: but according to the kindness that I have done unto thee, thou shalt do unto me, and to the land wherein thou hast sojourned. And Abraham said, I will swear. And Abraham reproved Abimelech because of a well of water, which

Abimelech's servants had violently taken away. And Abimelech said, I know not who hath done this thing: neither didst thou tell me, neither yet heard I of it, but today. And Abraham took sheep and oxen, and gave them unto Abimelech; and both of them made a covenant.

And Abraham set seven ewe lambs of the flock by themselves. And Abimelech said unto Abraham, What mean these seven ewe lambs which thou hast set by themselves? And he said, For these seven ewe lambs shalt thou take of my hand, that they may be a witness unto me, that I have digged this well. Wherefore he called that place Beersheba; because there they sware both of them. Thus they made a covenant at Beersheba: then Abimelech rose up, and Phichol the chief captain of his host, and they returned into the land of the Philistines. And Abraham planted a grove in Beersheba, and called there on the name of the Lord, the everlasting God. And Abraham sojourned in the Philistines' land many days. GENESIS 21

In chapters 17 and 18, God was revealed as the Almighty—the One who carries out His promises in spite of the weakness of His people and the wickedness of the world. In chapter 19, the evil of the world was fully demonstrated, while in chapter 20 the evil of the flesh and the weakness of God's people were manifested.

The world and the flesh having been exposed, we learn in chapter 21 that God's set time had come and the long promised heir was born (vv. 1-7); the bondwoman and her child were cast out (vv. 8-21); and the world had to acknowledge that God was with the man of faith (vv. 22-34).

THE BIRTH OF ISAAC (VV. 1-5)

Everything on man's side having broken down, we learn

that the *"set time of which God had spoken"* had come and the promised heir was born. He was called Isaac, meaning "laughter," and in due time was circumcised in accordance with the directions of the Lord. Everything takes place in God's set time and according to God's Word.

In the birth of Isaac we have a striking type of Christ, of whom we read, *"When the fullness of the time was come, God sent forth His Son"* (Gal. 4:4). Christ is the One through whom all the blessings promised to Abraham were secured, whether for Israel, the direct seed, or for the Gentile nations.

THE EFFECT OF THAT BIRTH (vv. 6-9)

In the two incidents that follow, we see the effect of the birth of the heir. In the one scene there were those who rejoiced; in the other there were those who mocked. Again, do not these two incidents strikingly bring before us the two-fold effect of the birth of Christ? Sarah said, *"God hath made me to laugh, so that all that hear will laugh with me."* Time was when her laughter was the expression of her unbelief; now it was the overflow of the joy of her heart. Moreover, her faith recognized that the birth of the son was so wholly of God, lying so entirely outside the thoughts of man, that she asked, *"Who would have said unto Abraham, that Sarah should have given children suck?"* So impossible was this to nature that no man would have said it. Only God would have said it; and only One who is almighty could carry out what He said.

So when at last the Christ of God became Incarnate there were those who, in harmony with heaven, recognized the intervention of God and could rejoice over the birth of the long-promised heir. With joy Mary delighted to say, *"He that is mighty hath done to me great things."* Zacharias saw that God had visited His people, *"To perform the mercy*

*promised to our fathers, and to remember His holy
covenant; the oath which He swore to our father Abraham"*
—these and all *"that looked for redemption in Jerusalem"*
(Lk. 1:49, 68-73).

But if there were those who rejoiced at the birth of Isaac,
there were also those who mocked, and we see what called
forth their enmity. There came a day when *"a great feast"*
was made in honor of the heir. This honor to the heir
aroused the jealousy and enmity of those who had long
held a position in the household of Abraham.

So in the history of our Lord, it was the recognition of
His supreme and unrivaled place that drew forth the jealousy and enmity of religious flesh. The wise men from the
East worshipped Him as the King of the Jews. Immediately
all Jerusalem was troubled and Herod, the false king,
sought to kill the holy Child.

THE LESSON FOR US (v. 10)

There are, however, other lessons for us in this deeply
instructive scene. In the Epistle to the Galatians, the apostle
quotes the words uttered by Sarah to Abraham, *"Cast out
this bondwoman and her son: for the son of this bondwoman shall not be heir with my son, even with Isaac."*

In this passage the apostle uses Isaac, not as representative of Christ, but of believers—those who are the subjects
of sovereign grace. He says, *"We, brethren, as Isaac was,
are the children of promise."* Moreover, as he uses Isaac to
set forth all that we are as born of the Spirit, so he uses
Ishmael to set forth our old man—all that we are as born
after the flesh. He shows, too, that the man that is after the
flesh is entirely opposed to the man that is after the Spirit.
*"As then he that was born after the flesh persecuted him
that was born after the Spirit, even so it is now"* (Gal.
4:28-31).

THE TRUE CHARACTER OF THE FLESH (vv. 11-12)

Even as the coming of Christ into the world exposed all that man is by nature and awakened the enmity of the flesh, so in the history of our own souls the more Christ has His true place in our affections, the more we discover the true character of the flesh that is still in us. If we make Christ a feast—if we give Him His true place in our hearts—we discover there is present with us that old man that always seeks to intrude and exalt self. This raises the great question, Am I going to spare the flesh by gratifying, indulging and exalting self, or am I going to refuse the flesh that Christ may have the supreme place in my life?

The Corinthian believers were indulging the flesh in a worldly form; the Colossian saints were in danger of ministering to the flesh by religious ritual; while the Galatian assemblies were giving place to the flesh by legality. They were putting themselves under law as a rule of life. But so far from producing a Christ-like life they only developed the fleshly life with its vain glory, and envy, and strife. So the apostle says, *"Cast out the bondwoman and her son."*

We are to refuse the law as a rule of life and the flesh which it stirs up. It is not that the believer slights the law, or is indifferent to its moral requirements. Far from this; but he is to refuse to put himself under the principle of law. Christ hath made us free from the law as a means of obtaining blessing; and we are to stand fast in the liberty by which Christ has made us free, looking to Him to keep us moment by moment. How truly this was the experience of the Apostle Paul. Christ had the supreme place in his affections, for he could say, *"For to me to live is Christ."* The result was that he refused his own righteousness which was of the law, and had no confidence in the flesh (Phil. 1:21; 3:3). He cast out the bondwoman and her son.

To refuse the flesh will call for self-denial, and this involves suffering. So to cast out the bondwoman was *"grievous in Abraham's sight."* He was reminded, however, that all blessing was connected with Isaac. To deny oneself and follow Christ will entail a cross—or suffering, but it will lead to great blessing in association with Christ.

THE PICTURE OF ISRAEL

Hagar and Ishmael as wanderers in the wilderness, with the water spent, may set forth typically the present position of Israel as a result of seeking to obtain the blessing under law, and so rejecting Christ, the Promised Seed. The earthly people of God have become wanderers in the world. Yet Israel is still the object of God's providential care even as God provided for Hagar and her son.

THE TESTIMONY OF THE WORLD (vv. 22-24)

In the closing scene of the chapter, the man of the world acknowledged that God was with the man of faith that walked in separation from the world. Time was when the man of faith slipped and, acting in unbelief, came under the reproof of Abimelech. Now the promised heir had come and was given his rightful place by Abraham, and the bond-woman and her son were cast out. What was of God was recognized as supreme and all that was of the flesh had been refused, with the result that Abimelech had to acknowledge, *"God is with thee in all that thou doest."* Instead of reproving Abraham, as in former days, he was reproved by Abraham. Nor is it otherwise today.

If Christ has His true place in our lives, if we refuse the flesh, and by faith walk in true separation from the world, the result will be that even the world will see and admit that God is with us.

THE TRUE CHARACTER OF THE WORLD (vv. 25-34)

While the world may have to admit that God is with His people who walk in separation, nonetheless it will seek to deprive the people of God of their means of spiritual refreshment. It will seek to stop our wells. Like Abraham, we may resist the world's efforts and reprove the world for attempting such a thing; but, like Abraham, let us seek to mingle with our reproofs the spirit of grace that seeks to impart to the world something of our blessing as represented by the seven ewe lambs.

The closing verses would appear to present the climax of Abraham's spiritual history. We have seen that the world has to acknowledge that God is with him; now we see that Abraham was with God. He called on the name of the Lord, the everlasting God and lived as a pilgrim in the land.

> *God's ways are not like human ways,*
> *He wears such strange disguises;*
> *He tires us by His long delays,*
> *And then our faith surprises.*
> *While we in unbelief deplore,*
> *And wonder at His staying,*
> *He stands already at the door,*
> *To interrupt our praying.*
>
> *He takes a leader from the Nile,*
> *Where mother hands have laid him;*
> *Hides him in palaces the while,*
> *Till He has right arrayed him.*
> *He sends him to the desert's hush,*
> *With flocks and herds to wander;*
> *Then meets him in the burning bush,*
> *New mysteries to ponder.*

Why should we doubt His care and grace,
As though He had forgotten?
As though time's changes could efface
What love had once begotten?
As though He'd lost us from His thought
And moved on now without us,
Whose love has always goodness wrought,
And constant been about us? —J. E. R.

THIRTEEN

The Offering Up of Isaac

And it came to pass after these things, that God did tempt Abraham, and said unto him, Abraham: and he said, Behold, here I am. And He said, Take now thy son, thine only son Isaac, whom thou lovest, and get thee into the land of Moriah; and offer him there for a burnt offering upon one of the mountains which I will tell thee of.

And Abraham rose up early in the morning, and saddled his ass, and took two of his young men with him, and Isaac his son, and clave the wood for the burnt offering, and rose up, and went unto the place of which God had told him. Then on the third day Abraham lifted up his eyes, and saw the place afar off. And Abraham said unto his young men, Abide ye here with the ass; and I and the lad will go yonder and worship, and come again to you. And Abraham took the wood of the burnt offering, and laid it upon Isaac his son; and he took the fire in his hand, and a knife; and they went both of them together. And Isaac spake unto Abraham his father, and said, My father: and he said, Here am I, my son. And he said, Behold the fire and the wood: but where is the lamb for a burnt offering? And Abraham said, My son, God will provide Himself a lamb for a burnt offering: so they went both of them together.

And they came to the place which God had told him of;

and Abraham built an altar there, and laid the wood in order, and bound Isaac his son, and laid him on the altar upon the wood. And Abraham stretched forth his hand, and took the knife to slay his son. And the angel of the Lord called to him out of heaven, and said, Abraham, Abraham: and he said, Here am I. And he said, Lay not thine hand upon the lad, neither do thou any thing unto him: for now I know that thou fearest God, seeing thou hast not withheld thy son, thine only son from Me. And Abraham lifted up his eyes, and looked, and behold behind him a ram caught in a thicket by his horns: and Abraham went and took the ram, and offered him up for a burnt offering in the stead of his son. And Abraham called the name of that place Jehovah-jireh: as it is said to this day, In the mount of the Lord it shall be seen. And the angel of the Lord called unto Abraham out of heaven the second time, And said, By Myself have I sworn, saith the Lord, for because thou hast done this thing, and hast not withheld thy son, thine only son: that in blessing I will bless thee, and in multiplying I will multiply thy seed as the stars of the heaven, and as the sand which is upon the sea shore; and thy seed shall possess the gate of his enemies; and in thy seed shall all the nations of the earth be blessed; because thou hast obeyed My voice. So Abraham returned unto his young men, and they rose up and went together to Beersheba; and Abraham dwelt at Beersheba.

And it came to pass after these things, that it was told Abraham, saying, Behold, Milcah, she hath also born children unto thy brother Nahor…And his concubine, whose name was Reumah, she bare also Tebah, and Gaham, and Thahash, and Maachah.   GENESIS 22

The first portion of Abraham's life presented his public testimony as a man of faith walking in separation from the world, in answer to the call of God (chs. 12-14). In the second part of his history, commencing with the words, *"After these things,"* we learn the inner exercises of his soul in his personal relationships with God (chs. 15-21).

THE LAST PHASE OF ABRAHAM'S LIFE

With the twenty-second chapter of Genesis we enter on the last phase of his life. It also commenced with the words, *"After these things."* In this and the following chapters, there passes before us certain incidents which, in a very distinct way, set forth in type the ways of God in carrying out His purposes for the glory of Christ and the blessing of man.

In chapter 21, we saw in the birth of Isaac at *"the set time"* a foreshadowing of that great moment of which we read, *"when the fullness of the time was come, God sent forth His Son, made of a woman"* (Gal. 4:4). In chapter 22, we see a type of the death and resurrection of Christ—the Lamb of God's providing. In chapter 23, the death and burial of Sarah sets forth in type the setting aside of Israel, the earthly bride, in consequence of the rejection of Christ. In chapter 24, while Israel was set aside, we have the calling out of the Church—the heavenly bride, set forth in Rebekah.

While we seek to profit by the typical aspects of these striking incidents, we must not overlook their moral bearing. If this twenty-second chapter is a marvelous presentation of the love of God in giving the Son, morally it also sets forth in a striking way the faith of Abraham.

THE SUPREME TEST

The moral teaching comes before us in the opening words: *"And it came to pass after these things, that God tried Abraham"* (NEW TRANS.). In that great chapter in the

Epistle to the Hebrews which presents before us those who have trodden the path of faith, we find that Abraham has an outstanding place. It is not only that he is presented as one who by faith answered the call of God, but he is highly privileged as having his faith tested beyond that of any man before or since. In the account we read that God said to him, *"Take now thy son, thine only son, Isaac, whom thou lovest, and get thee into the land of Moriah: and offer him there for a burnt offering."* The inspired comment in Hebrews is, *"By faith Abraham, when he was tried, offered up Isaac,"* the very one in whom all the promises centered, and of whom it was said, *"That in Isaac shall thy seed be called."* He was told to do that which to natural reason would make the fulfillment of the promises of God impossible. But we learn that he acted, not according to mere reason, but *"by faith...accounting that God was able to raise him up, even from the dead; from whence he received him in a figure."*

The Act of Obedience

When Job's children were taken from him, he graciously submitted to what God had allowed, for he said, *"The Lord gave and the Lord hath taken away."* But Abraham's faith was tried with a much severer test, and rises to a far higher level. He was not simply asked to submit passively to the will of God, but was called to take part actively in that which was contrary to nature, extreme anguish to a father's heart. And apart from God's direction, it would have been an outrage against the laws of God and man. But Abraham, with God-given faith, answered to the test. With calm deliberation, he rose up early in the morning, saddled his ass, and taking two young men and Isaac his son, he *"went unto the place of which God had told him."*

For three days he traveled on his way. Time and

opportunity was thus given to thoroughly enter into what he was called to do. For three days this terrible trial was before his soul. During these days he had to face the agony of offering up his son. It was not an act hurriedly done under some momentary impulse. It was deliberately done after having entered into all that it cost him. His love to his son, the feelings of Isaac and his love to his father, God's promise that *"in Isaac shall thy seed be called"*—all was fully faced, but faith triumphed.

Had unbelief been at work, there was time given to turn back. But faith persevered, and on the third day, the place having come in sight, he *"said unto his young men, Abide ye here with the ass; and I and the lad will go yonder and worship, and come again to you."* Faith, accounting that God can raise the dead, can say with the utmost confidence, we will *"come again."*

We are not tested in the same manner as Abraham, but it is a good thing if we can say when our loved ones are taken, *"if we believe that Jesus died and rose again, even so them also which sleep in Jesus will God bring with Him."* Faith knows that though for a time they are taken from us—and have gone yonder to worship—they will *"come again."*

FATHER AND SON

Isaac inquired, *"Where is the lamb for a burnt offering"* In faith Abraham replied, *"My son, God will provide Himself a lamb; "* and without further word, they passed on *"both of them together."* Without resistance or complaint, Isaac submitted to be bound to the altar and Abraham *"stretched forth his hand...to slay his son."*

Then in the nick of time the angel of the Lord intervened. Abraham's hand was withheld from plunging the knife into his son. Abraham's faith had answered to the test and God says, *"Now I know that thou fearest God, seeing thou hast not withheld thy son, thine only son from Me."* Acting in the fear of God, he overcame the fear of man in doing that which man would have utterly condemned.

ANOTHER FATHER—ANOTHER SON

Viewing this remarkable scene in its typical bearing, there rises up before us the greatness of the love of God in giving His Son to die for us. The word to Abraham is *"take now thy son,"* telling us that God *"spared not His own Son, but delivered Him up for us all"* (Rom. 8:32). Then Abraham was told that he was to take his *"only son."* Three times in the chapter is it emphasized that Isaac was his *"only"* son (vv. 2, 12, 16). Again this speaks of the love of God by which *"He gave His only begotten Son"* (Jn. 3:16). Further, Abraham is reminded that the son he is to offer up was one *"whom thou lovest,"* speaking to us of the fact that Christ is the One of whom it is said, *"The Father loveth the Son"* (Jn. 3:35). It is significant that this, the first mention of love in the Bible, is in connection with a scene that speaks of the love of a father for his son.

PERFECT OBEDIENCE

Moreover, if the scene brings before us the love of God in giving the Son, so also it presents the perfect submission and uncomplaining obedience to his father's will. In all this there is the bright foreshadowing of the perfect obedience of Christ to the Father which led Him to say in view of death, *"Not My will, but Thine be done"* (Lk. 22:42).

During the three days' journey the wood of the burnt offering was borne by Isaac while the fire and the knife were in the hand of Abraham. Throughout the years of His ministry the Lord bore the knowledge of His coming death. Over every step of His way there was the shadow of the cross. The crowds may wonder at *"all things which Jesus did,"* but He knew that the Son of Man would be delivered into the hands of men (Lk. 9:44). The apostles may follow Him to Jerusalem with visions of the Kingdom being set up in power, and Christ reigning on a throne of glory, but He knew that He was moving towards the shameful cross.

Nevertheless, if men were allowed to crucify the Lord, the fire and the knife—speaking of judgment and death— were in the hands of God. Men may think that they can crucify, or release the Lord according to their will, but the Lord can say to Pilate, *"Thou couldest have no power at all against Me except it were given thee from above"* (Jn. 19:11). No eye could pierce the darkness of that great scene when the fire and the knife fell upon Christ. But all that took place then was received from God's hand, for Christ could say, *"Thou hast laid Me in the lowest pit, in darkness, in the deeps. Thy wrath lieth hard upon Me, and Thou hast afflicted Me with all Thy waves"* (Ps. 88:6-7).

Perfect Communion

There came a moment when the "young men" were left behind and Abraham and his only son went up alone to the mount. This surely speaks to us of that great moment of which the Lord has to say, *"Whither I go, thou canst not follow Me now"* (Jn. 13:36). And yet the Lord can say, *"He that sent Me is with Me: the Father hath not left Me alone"* (Jn. 8:29). Thus, of Abraham and Isaac we twice read, *"They went both of them together"* (vv. 6, 8), speaking to us of the perfect communion of the Father and the Son presented in the Gospel of John as the Lord Jesus moved forward to the cross to become the great burnt offering by which God is perfectly glorified. The Lord could say, *"My Father worketh hitherto and I work"*; again, *"I seek not Mine own will, but the will of the Father which hath sent*

Me." Later He can say, *"I do always those things that please Him"*; and again, *"I and My Father are one"* (Jn. 5:17, 30; 8:29; 10:30).

PERFECT SUBMISSION

Arriving at the place, Isaac was perfectly submissive to the one that was called to act. Abraham built the altar; Abraham laid the wood in order: Abraham bound Isaac, his son; Abraham laid him upon the altar, and Abraham stretched forth his hand and took the knife to slay his son. So of Christ we read, *"He opened not His mouth: He is brought as a lamb to the slaughter, and as a sheep before her shearers is dumb, so He openeth not His mouth...Yet it pleased the Lord to bruise Him; He hath put Him to grief"* (Isa. 53:7-10).

COMPARISON AND CONTRAST

It is significant that in all the offerings, the victim was first killed and then laid on the altar. Here the offering becomes a more striking type of Christ in that he was first bound to the altar before the knife was taken to slay him.

But every type must fall short of the reality. In the type the angel of the Lord arrested the hand that held the knife, and Isaac was spared. At the cross no hand was put forth to stay the power of death. The love of the Father spared not the Son, and the love of the Son submitted to the Father's will in going into death. An angel might strengthen the Lord in the garden, but there was no angel to shelter from judgment at the cross.

In a figure, Abraham received Isaac from the dead (Heb. 11:19). But if Isaac was to go free, death must come on the ram caught in the thicket—a further type of the Lamb of God's providing. In the course of this wonderful scene Abraham uttered the two prophetic statements: first, *"God will provide Himself a Lamb for a burnt offering"*; secondly, *"In the mount of the Lord it shall be provided"* (NKJV). As the Lord could say, *"Abraham rejoiced to see My day: and he saw it, and was glad"* (Jn. 8:56).

God renewed His promises to Abraham on the ground of sacrifice, and confirmed His promise of blessing to all the nations of the earth through the risen seed. Here we know, from the Epistle to the Galatians, that the seed is Christ, for, says the apostle, *"To Abraham and his seed were the promises made. He saith not, And to seeds, as of many; but as of one, And to thy seed, which is Christ"* (Gal. 3:16).

The genealogy of the closing verses seems purposely given at this point to introduce Rebekah, the one that so blessedly sets forth the heavenly bride of Christ.

O blessed Lord, what hast Thou done!
How vast a ransom paid!
God's only well-beloved Son
Upon the altar laid!

The Father in His willing love
Could spare Thee from His side;
And Thou couldst stoop to bear above,
At such a cost, Thy bride.

While our full hearts in faith repose
Upon Thy precious blood,
Peace in a steady current flows,
Filled from Thy mercy's flood.

What boundless joy will fill each heart,
Our every grief efface,
When we behold Thee as Thou art,
And all Thy love retrace.

Unseen we love Thee, dear Thy name!
But when our eyes behold,
With joyful wonder we'll proclaim,
"The half hath not been told!"

For Thou exceedest all the fame
Our ears have ever heard;
How happy we who know Thy name,
And trust Thy faithful Word!

The Lamb of God to slaughter led,
The King of Glory see!
The crown of thorns upon His head,
They nail Him to the tree!

The Father gives His only Son;
The Lord of glory dies
For us, the guilty and undone,
A spotless Sacrifice!

Thy Name is holy, O our God!
Before Thy throne we bow;
Thy bosom is Thy saints' abode,
We call Thee Father now!

Enthroned with Thee now sits the Lord,
And in Thy bosom dwells;
Justice, that smote Him with the sword,
Our perfect pardon seals.

Eternal death was once our doom;
Now death hast lost its sting;
We rose with Jesus from the tomb,
Jehovah's love to sing. —R. C. CHAPMAN

FOURTEEN

The Death of Sarah

And Sarah was an hundred and seven and twenty years old: these were the years of the life of Sarah. And Sarah died in Kirjath-arba; the same is Hebron in the land of Canaan: and Abraham came to mourn for Sarah, and to weep for her. And Abraham stood up from before his dead, and spake unto the sons of Heth, saying, I am a stranger and a sojourner with you: give me a possession of a buryingplace with you, that I may bury my dead out of my sight.

And the children of Heth answered Abraham, saying unto him, Hear us, my lord: thou art a mighty prince among us: in the choice of our sepulchers bury thy dead; none of us shall withhold from thee his sepulcher, but that thou mayest bury thy dead.

And Abraham stood up, and bowed himself to the people of the land, even to the children of Heth. And he communed with them, saying, If it be your mind that I should bury my dead out of my sight; hear me, and intreat for me to Ephron the son of Zohar, that he may give me the cave of Machpelah, which he hath, which is in the end of his field; for as much money as it is worth he shall give it me for a possession of a buryingplace amongst you.

And Ephron dwelt among the children of Heth: and Ephron the Hittite answered Abraham in the audience of the children of Heth, even of all that went in at the gate of his city, saying, Nay, my lord, hear me: the field give I thee, and the cave that is therein, I give it thee; in the presence of the sons of my people give I it thee: bury thy dead. And Abraham bowed down himself before the people of the land. And he spake unto Ephron in the audience of the people of the land, saying, But if thou wilt give it, I pray thee, hear me: I will give thee money for the field; take it of me, and I will bury my dead there.

And Ephron answered Abraham, saying unto him, My lord, hearken unto me: the land is worth four hundred shekels of silver; what is that betwixt me and thee? bury therefore thy dead.

And Abraham hearkened unto Ephron; and Abraham weighed to Ephron the silver, which he had named in the audience of the sons of Heth. four hundred shekels of silver, current money with the merchant. And the field of Ephron, which was in Machpelah, which was before Mamre, the field, and the cave which was therein, and all the trees that were in the field, that were in all the borders round about, were made sure unto Abraham for a possession in the presence of the children of Heth, before all that went in at the gate of his city.

And after this, Abraham buried Sarah his wife in the cave of the field of Machpelah before Mamre: the same is Hebron in the land of Canaan. And the field, and the cave that is therein, were made sure unto Abraham for a possession of a buryingplace by the sons of Heth.   GENESIS 23

In chapter 23 we have the record of the death and burial of Sarah. As so often, in these Old Testament histories, the facts related have a typical as well as a moral significance.

That this is no fanciful conclusion is clear from the twofold interpretation of these events given in the New Testament.

AN ALLEGORY

In the Epistle to the Galatians the apostle gives us the allegorical significance of Hagar and Sarah. Hagar and her son represent the law and those who are seeking blessing under law; while Sarah and her children represent the unconditional promises of God and those who are blessed through grace (Gal. 4:21-26). The people of Israel, having put themselves under law, sought to obtain blessing on the ground of their own efforts; the result being they only brought forth the evil works of the flesh. They rejected Christ who was presented to them in grace, and through whom they could have received blessing on the ground of the promises made to Abraham. Peter, addressing the nation after the death and resurrection of Christ, could say, *"Ye are the children of the prophets, and of the covenant which God made with our fathers, saying unto Abraham, And in thy seed shall all the kindreds of the earth be blessed. Unto you first God, having raised up His Son Jesus, sent Him to bless you, in turning away every one of you from his iniquities"* (Acts 3:25-26). This offer of grace was rejected by the nation, and as a result, for the time being, God's earthly people are set aside.

CHRIST'S EARTHLY BRIDE

The death of Sarah, following the offering up of Isaac, would seem to bring before us this setting aside of the nation of Israel that followed their rejection of the grace offered to them on the ground of the death and resurrection of Christ. Sarah, type of the wife of Jehovah, passes from the story, and Rebekah, type of the heavenly bride, comes into view.

A Plain Declaration

Such then would appear to be the typical meaning of the death and burial of Sarah. There is, however, the moral significance of these incidents, so clearly brought before us in the Epistle to the Hebrews. There we learn that these saints of old not only lived by faith but they *"all died in faith, not having received the promises, but having seen them afar off, and were persuaded of them, and embraced them, and confessed that they were strangers and pilgrims on the earth. For they that say such things declare plainly that they seek a country"* (Heb. 11:13-14).

Here, then, we see the faith of Abraham in the presence of death; the confession that he was but a stranger and a pilgrim, and, by his actions, declaring plainly his pilgrim character before the world.

Faith's Prospect

Abraham's faith had received Isaac at the word of the Lord when his own body was as good as dead. His faith had offered up Isaac at the word of the Lord, accounting that God was able to raise him up even from the dead. Then, in like faith, he buried Sarah in the sure and certain hope of resurrection. In faith he had ascended Mount Moriah to offer up his son. In like faith he now faced the cave of Machpelah to bury his wife. The moment had come when he had to bury his *"dead out of sight,"* but his faith knew that his loved one would come again and have her part in that better, heavenly country to which his faith was looking on.

The God of Resurrection

God had revealed Himself to Abraham as the Almighty, and as the God of resurrection, and had assured him that the land wherein he was a stranger—all the land of Canaan —was given to him for an everlasting possession (17:8). All was his by promise, though not yet in possession. In the faith of God's promise he was careful to lay the body of Sarah to rest in the Promised Land. In the land of Canaan she had lived with Abraham as a stranger and a pilgrim; *"in the land of Canaan"* she had died; and *"in the land of Canaan"* she was buried (vv. 2, 19). In the same faith, at a later date, the sons of Isaac bury their father at Hebron, in the land of Canaan (Gen. 35:27-29). So, too, in due time, Jacob, though he died in Egypt, was buried in faith by his sons in the land of Canaan, in the cave of Machpelah (Gen. 50:13). An similarly, Joseph when he came to die, took an oath of the children of Israel that they should carry his bones from Egypt to the land of Canaan (Gen. 50:25-26; Ex. 13:19).

GODLY SORROW

If, however, in these scenes we see shining examples of the faith of God's elect in the presence of death, we also learn that faith does not set aside natural affection. Thus we read, *"Abraham came to mourn for Sarah, and to weep for her"* (v. 2). Faith knows full well that our loved ones that die in the Lord will rise again, and that for them death is gain; nonetheless we rightly mourn and feel their loss. Our sure and certain hope of resurrection tells us, as the apostle reminds us, that our sorrow is not the sorrow of those who have no hope. But there is no word to say we are not to sorrow. None could know the power of resurrection like the One who is Himself the resurrection and the life, and yet He wept at the grave of Lazarus.

A PROMISE FULFILLED

Furthermore, we see that in the presence of death,

Abraham still acted as suits one that was a stranger and a pilgrim. He confessed before the sons of Heth, *"I am a stranger and a sojourner with you."* As such he gained the respect of the world, for they said, *"Thou art a prince of God among us"* (v. 6, NEW TRANS.). How striking the contrast to poor Lot—the believer who gave up his pilgrim character to dwell in Sodom. Such an example the world treats with well-merited contempt, for in the day of his trouble they said, *"Stand back...this one fellow came in to sojourn, and he will needs be a judge"* (19:9). Sixty years before this God had said to Abraham that one result of answering to the call of God, and taking the outside place, would be that God would make his name great (Gen. 12:2). Here we see this word fulfilled, for the very world had to acknowledge that this separate man was *"a mighty prince of God."* Poor Lot, who sought to make himself great in the world, as a judge in the gate, had to *"stand back"* and take a place of contempt in the eyes of the world.

A LOWLY MIND

Nevertheless, Abraham did not presume upon the high respect in which he was held by the world in order to exalt himself. He did not speak of his dignities, of his high calling, or of the glories that lie before him. In the days of the Lord, when the careless world would make Him a King, He made Himself of no reputation and departed into a mountain alone (Jn. 6:15). In like spirit, Abraham refused to magnify himself. He did not seek that the world should bow to him as a mighty prince, but rather he was marked by the lowly mind, for twice we read, he *"bowed himself to the people of the land"* (vv. 7-12).

A RIGHTEOUS CHARACTER

The kindness of the world would press upon Abraham a

burying place as a gift. True to his pilgrim character he refused to take the place of a prince that receives gifts, and was content to be the stranger that paid for his wants. He refused to use the praise of the world to exalt himself, and he would not let the kindness of the world move him from the path of strangership. As before he had refused the gifts of the king of Sodom, so he also declined the gifts of the children of Heth. He bought the burying place, and as becomes a stranger in all his dealings with the world, he acted in strict righteousness paying *"four hundred shekels of silver, current money with the merchant."*

In all these ways we see that Abraham in his day was one that called on the Lord out of a pure heart, and followed righteousness, faith, love, and peace.

Midst the darkness, storm and sorrow, one bright gleam I see:
Well I know the blessed morrow Christ will come for me.
Midst the light and peace and glory of the Father's home,
Christ for me is watching, waiting—waiting till I come.

Long the blessed Guide has led me by the desert road;
Now I see the golden towers—City of my God.
There amidst the love and glory, He is waiting yet;
On His hands a name is graven He can ne'er forget.

There amidst the songs of heaven, sweeter to His ear
Is the footfall through the desert, ever drawing near.
There, made ready are the mansions, glorious, bright, and fair;
But the Bride the Father gave Him still is wanting there.

Who is this who comes to meet me on the desert way,
As the morning star foretelling God's unclouded day?
He it is who came to win me on the cross of shame;
In His glory well I know Him, evermore the same.

Oh, the blessed joy of meeting, all the desert past!
Oh, the wondrous words of greeting He shall speak at last!
He and I together ent'ring those bright courts above;
He and I together sharing all the Father's love.

Where no shade nor stain can enter, nor the gold be dim;
In that holiness unsullied I shall walk with Him.
Meet companion then for Jesus, from Him, for Him made;
Glory of God's grace forever there in me displayed.

He who in His hour of sorrow bore the curse alone;
I who through the lonely desert trod where He had gone.
He and I in that bright glory one deep joy shall share:
Mine, to be forever with Him; His, that I am there.

FIFTEEN

The Call of Rebekah

And Abraham was old, and well stricken in age: and the Lord had blessed Abraham in all things. And Abraham said unto his eldest servant of his house, that ruled over all that he had, Put, I pray thee, thy hand under my thigh: And I will make thee swear by the Lord, the God of heaven, and the God of the earth, that thou shalt not take a wife unto my son of the daughters of the Canaanites, among whom I dwell: but thou shalt go unto my country, and to my kindred, and take a wife unto my son Isaac.

And the servant said unto him, Peradventure the woman will not be willing to follow me unto this land: must I needs bring thy son again unto the land from whence thou camest? And Abraham said unto him, Beware thou that thou bring not my son thither again. The Lord God of heaven, which took me from my father's house, and from the land of my kindred, and which spake unto me, and that sware unto me, saying, Unto thy seed will I give this land; He shall send His angel before thee, and thou shalt take a wife unto my son from thence…And the servant put his hand under the thigh of Abraham his master, and sware to him concerning that matter.

And the servant took ten camels of the camels of his master, and departed…and he arose, and went to

Meso-potamia, unto the city of Nahor...And he said, O Lord God of my master Abraham, I pray thee, send me good speed this day, and show kindness unto my master Abraham. Behold, I stand here by the well of water; and the daughters of the men of the city come out to draw water: and let it come to pass, that the damsel to whom I shall say, Let down thy pitcher, I pray thee, that I may drink; and she shall say, Drink, and I will give thy camels drink also: let the same be she that thou hast appointed for thy servant Isaac; and thereby shall I know that thou hast showed kindness unto my master.

And it came to pass, before he had done speaking, that, behold, Rebekah came out, who was born to Bethuel, son of Milcah, the wife of Nahor, Abraham's brother, with her pitcher upon her shoulder. And the damsel was very fair to look upon, a virgin, neither had any man known her: and she went down to the well, and filled her pitcher, and came up. And the servant ran to meet her, and said, Let me, I pray thee, drink a little water of thy pitcher. And she said, Drink, my lord: and she hasted, and let down her pitcher upon her hand, and gave him drink. And when she had done giving him drink, she said, I will draw water for thy camels also, until they have done drinking...

She said moreover unto him, We have both straw and provender enough, and room to lodge in. And the man bowed down his head, and worshiped the Lord. And he said, Blessed be the Lord God of my master Abraham, who hath not left destitute my master of his mercy and his truth. I being in the way, the Lord led me to the house of my master's brethren. GENESIS 24:1-27

In the offering up of Isaac, recorded in chapter 22, we cannot fail to see a striking type of the death and resurrection of Christ. Then, in chapter 23, the death and burial of

Sarah typifies the setting aside of Israel—God's earthly people—that followed upon their rejection of Christ. In this chapter there is a beautiful picture of the calling out of the Church that takes place during the time Israel is set aside.

THREE GREAT TRUTHS

We know that after the death and resurrection of Christ, He ascended to glory and took His place at the right hand of God. Then there followed that great event, the coming of the Holy Spirit—a divine Person—to dwell with and in believers on earth. These three great truths mark the day in which we live: first, that there is a Man in the glory, Christ Jesus; secondly, there is a divine Person on earth, the Holy Spirit; thirdly, the Holy Spirit has come to form the Church, to guide her through this world, and to present her to Christ in the day of His coming glory.

A COMPREHENSIVE VIEW

These are the great truths that pass before us in type in Genesis 24. The immense importance of the chapter lies in the fact that it presents in a picture what each divine Person in the Godhead is engaged in during the day in which we live. As we look around we see the increasing wickedness of the world, and the increasing failure and weakness of the people of God. Looking upon all this confusion, we can easily become depressed and cast down. When, however, we look at the picture presented in this chapter, we see in a comprehensive view what God is doing to carry out His own purposes. Other scriptures may bring into prominence the faith as well as the failure of believers for our encouragement and warning. But here comes before us in all its blessedness what God is effecting for the glory of Christ, in spite of every adverse influence, whether in ourselves, in the world, or by the devil.

Seeing what God is doing, and the object that He has before Him, and knowing that all that God has purposed He will assuredly carry out, will keep the soul at rest in the midst of a scene of turmoil. Moreover, it will make us intelligent in the mind of God and save us from disappointment from false expectations. Further, we shall be saved from expending our energies in so many activities that, while they have the benefit of the world in view, are wholly outside the purpose of God.

In the course of the story there comes before us three main subjects: first, the directions of Abraham to his servant (vv. 1-9); secondly, the mission of the servant in Mesopotamia (vv. 10-61); and thirdly, the meeting between Isaac and Rebekah in the land of Canaan (vv. 62-67).

THE FATHER'S PURPOSE

Abraham's directions very beautifully set forth the counsels of God the Father concerning the Son, and what God is doing in the world today by the Holy Spirit in carrying out His purposes.

First, we learn that the great object of the servant's mission was, as Abraham said, to *"take a wife unto my son."* The servant was sent to Mesopotamia with this single object in view. Having found the bride and brought her to Isaac, his mission would be accomplished. It was no part of the servant's work to interfere with the political or social interests of Mesopotamia. The Holy Spirit is not here to improve or reform the world, or bring peace to the nations, or even convert the world. He is not here to right the wrongs of the poor, remove oppression, or relieve man from disease, want, and misery.

There is One that in due time will indeed bring peace and blessing to the world. One who has been here and proved that He had the power and grace to relieve man of every pressure. Alas! we nailed Him to a cross, and He is gone, so the misery of the world remains. Nevertheless, He is coming again to bring in the blessing. But in the meantime Jesus is in heaven and the Holy Spirit is down here to obtain the bride for Christ—a heavenly people—and conduct her to Christ in the gloryland.

Christendom, unfortunately, has so entirely missed the mind of God that it looks at Christianity as merely a religious system for the improvement and uplifting of man, in order to make the world a better and brighter place. If this is all that people see in Christianity, little wonder that they are giving up its profession, for it is evident that after nineteen centuries the world grows worse rather than better, and today it is filled with increasing violence and corruption, and men's hearts are failing them with fear of things coming upon the earth.

It is true that God in His providence cares for His poor creatures and can, and does, restrain the evil of men. It is also true that where the truth is received it will certainly bring a measure of improvement in temporal circumstances. But with our thoughts directed by the Word of God, we see that the Holy Spirit is here to take a people out of the world for Christ in glory.

The servant was told that the bride for Isaac was not to be of the daughters of the Canaanites. Abraham said she was to be of *"my kindred."* The Canaanites were under the curse and devoted to judgment. In the same way, there can be no link between Christ in the glory and a world under judgment. Isaac's bride was not to be a stranger but one that already belonged to Abraham's family. So the Church is formed not of unbelievers, nor of a mixture of believers and unbelievers, but wholly of the family of faith.

Further, the servant was warned that in no case was he to bring Isaac back to Mesopotamia. During the time that the servant was in Mesopotamia, Isaac was in Canaan, and there was no link between Isaac and the people of Mesopotamia. So we know today that there is no direct link between Christ in heaven and the world as such. Failing to see this, the efforts of Christendom—as well as of many sincere Christians—are entirely directed to doing the very thing that the servant is twice warned not to do. The attempt is made (in a variety of different forms) to bring Christ back to the world and attach His Name to benevolent schemes for the reformation and improvement of the world. Such efforts are entirely outside the work of the Spirit who is here not to bring Christ back to the world but to take a people out of the world for Christ.

It is true that in due time Christ is coming back to the world, but let us not forget that the last time the world saw Christ, He was on the cross to which they had nailed Him. The next time they see Him will be when He comes *"in flaming fire taking vengeance on them that know not God, and that obey not the gospel of our Lord Jesus Christ"* (2 Thess. 1:7-9).

Finally, the servant was told that God's angel would go before him. We know that the angels are *"ministering spirits sent forth to minister for them who shall be heirs of salvation."* Their service always seems to be of a providential and guardian character. The Holy Spirit deals with souls, while the angels seem to act in relation to circumstances. An angel may have directed Philip as to the way he should take, but the Spirit directed him in dealing with a soul (Acts 8:26, 29).

THE SERVANT'S MISSION

This part of the story is rich with instruction for us seeing that it typically presents not only the object of the Spirit's coming but also the way He carries out this object.

The servant came to Mesopotamia well-equipped for his service, for we read, *"All the goods of his master were in his hand,"* reminding us that the Holy Spirit has come to teach us *"all things,"* to guide us into *"all truth,"* and show us *"all things that the Father hath"* (Jn. 14:26; 16:13-15).

The servant's work in Mesopotamia had a fourfold character: first, he found the bride appointed for Isaac (vv. 10-21); secondly, having found the bride, he distinguished her from all others (v. 22); thirdly, he weaned her heart from Mesopotamia, and attached her affections to Isaac (vv. 23-53); finally, he led her across the desert to her unseen bridegroom (vv. 54-61).

<h3 align="center">THE BRIDE FOUND</h3>

We learn from the prayer of the servant the great purpose of his mission. He did not pray for the men of the city, or their daughters; he was engrossed with one object—to find the bride appointed for Isaac.

Moreover, we see that the infallible sign of the appointed bride was that she would be marked by grace. The servant prayed, *"Let it come to pass, that the damsel to whom I shall say, Let down thy pitcher, I pray thee, that I may drink; and she shall say, Drink, and I will give thy camels drink also: let the same be she that Thou hast appointed for Thy servant Isaac"* (Gen. 24:14).

The prayer was granted, for when Rebekah arrived at the well and was put to the test, she answered the servant's request, and said, *"I will draw for thy camels also."* In all this we are reminded of the Spirit working in grace in those who are the *"elect according to the foreknowledge of God the Father through sanctification of the Spirit"* (1 Pet. 1:2).

<h3 align="center">THE BRIDE ADORNED</h3>

Secondly, the servant, having found the appointed bride

was not content with a work of grace which only he could see, but he publicly distinguished the bride from all others by adorning her with the golden earrings and the bracelets of gold, which others could see. Not only is the Spirit here to produce a work of grace in the believer, but there is to be seen in the believer the fruits of being sealed by the Spirit—love, joy, peace, longsuffering, kindness, goodness, fidelity, meekness, and temperance. These precious jewels are a witness to others, and distinguish the believer from the world around.

THE STORY TOLD

Thirdly, we see the pains that the servant took to link the affections of Rebekah with Isaac. Again, this sets forth the work of the Spirit by which believers are strengthened in the inner man in order that Christ may dwell in their hearts by faith. This part of the servant's work was introduced by the question, *"Is there room in thy father's house for us to lodge in?"* Rebekah's answer again went beyond the servant's request. He only asked for *"room"*; she said that there was *"provision"* as well as room (v. 25). Laban, too, could say to the servant, *"Come in, thou blessed of the Lord."* So we read, *"The man came into the house"* (vv. 31-32). The Holy Spirit has come to take of the things of Christ and show them unto us (Jn. 16:14). But we do well to take home to ourselves this great question, *"Is there room?"* Are we prepared to put ourselves out to make room for the Holy Spirit? The flesh and the Spirit *"are contrary the one to the other"* (Gal. 5:17). We cannot entertain the Spirit if ministering to the flesh. To make room for the Spirit while at the same time to be minding the things of the flesh is impossible. Are we prepared to refuse the indulgence of the flesh in the passing things of time in order to make room for the Spirit to lead us into the deep and eternal things of God? Are we making room and provision for the Spirit? *"Room"* and *"provision"* were made in the house of Bethuel for the servant of Abraham with the result that the servant was able to speak of Isaac, to engage the affections of Rebekah with Isaac, and lead her to Isaac.

THE BRIDE WON

Having been warmly welcomed into the house, at once the servant bore witness to Isaac. He revealed the mind of his master concerning Isaac, and in so doing he took of the things of Isaac and showed them to Rebekah. He spoke of the wealth of his master, and showed that all was given to Isaac: *"Unto him hath he given all that he hath."* So the Lord Himself tells us that *"All things that the Father hath are Mine,"* and that the work of the Spirit will be to take of His things and show them to us (Jn. 16:15).

THE RESPONSE

Having spoken of Isaac and the purpose of Abraham for the blessing of Isaac, the servant paused to see the effect of his message. Does not the Spirit deal with us in like manner? Does He not wait to see if we respond to His unfoldings of Christ before He makes us a public witness to Christ? In the picture there was a ready response, with the result that at once *"the servant brought forth jewels of silver, and jewels of gold, and raiment, and gave them to Rebekah."* In the same way, if we respond to the unfoldings of the Spirit concerning Christ, He will make us the witnesses of redeeming love—the jewels of silver; the witnesses of divine righteousness—the jewels of gold; and the witnesses of practical sanctification—the raiment.

THE DECISION MADE

Finally, having engaged the affections of Rebekah with

Isaac, the servant's one great aim was to lead Rebekah to Isaac. The servant said, *"Send me away unto my master."* He had come to find the bride, and having accomplished that end, he longed to be away. He had not come to find the bride and settle her in her old home, but to lead her to a new home.

The relatives wanted to detain Rebekah at least ten days. The servant's desire was to be away, and by his report of Isaac, he formed the same mind in Rebekah. If we allow the Holy Spirit to have His way with us—if we hinder Him not—He will form our minds according to His mind, to think as He thinks about Christ, to detach our hearts from the things where Christ is not, and to engage our affections with Christ where He is. Too often we hinder the work of the Spirit by clinging to the world, its politics, its pleasures, and its religion. But the world cannot hold us if our hearts are set on reaching Christ in glory.

Earthly relations may have sought to detain Rebekah, but after all, the decision rested with her. They said, *"We will call the damsel and enquire at her mouth."* So the great question for Rebekah was, *"Wilt thou go with this man?"* This is still the question for each one of us. Do we recognize the presence of the Holy Spirit, and are we prepared at all cost to follow His leading?

Christendom has almost entirely ignored the presence of the Spirit, with the result that multitudes who take Christ's name have settled down in the world that has rejected Him and from which He is absent. It is a great moment when our hearts are so attached to Christ in heaven that, like Rebekah, we say, *"I will go."*

A PATHWAY FOLLOWED

The immediate result of her decision was that *"they sent away Rebekah their sister, and her nurse, and Abraham's servant and his men."* If we let it be known that we are forgetting the things that are behind and have set our hearts on heavenly things, it will not be simply a question of our giving up the world. The world will give us up; we shall be *"sent away."*

Then we read that *"Rebekah arose...and followed the man; and the servant took Rebekah, and went his way."* Believers, while gladly submitting to God's way of salvation, often are tempted to go their own way to heaven. Our desire should be to know *"His way"* and to follow as He leads. To follow the Spirit will not be to follow some inner light, as men speak, but will be to walk according to the Word of God. And the Spirit, using the Word of God, will always gather us to Christ.

Thus Rebekah, following the man, found herself on a wilderness journey. For the moment she had neither the home of Laban nor the home of Isaac. So if we follow the leading of the Spirit, we shall find that "we have neither the earth in which we are, nor heaven to which we are going." Nevertheless, as Rebekah traveled the four hundred miles of desert journey, she had a bright prospect before her. At the end, Isaac—to whom her heart had been attached—was waiting to receive her.

In like spirit the Apostle Paul can say, *"One thing I do, forgetting those things which are behind, and reaching forth unto those things which are before, I pursue, looking towards the goal for the prize of the calling on high of God in Christ Jesus"* (Phil. 3:13-14, NEW TRANS.).

THE GOAL REACHED

The servant in Mesopotamia throughout his mission always had in view the great day when the bride, having been guided across the desert, would be presented to Isaac. In all these events Isaac had taken no active part, nor had he left the land of Canaan. All was left in the hands of the servant. Nevertheless, Isaac was far from indifferent to the mission of the servant and the coming of the bride. At evening Isaac came from the way of the well Lahai-roi to meet the bride. The significant meaning of the well is said to be *"the well of Him that liveth and seeth."* If this is so, it would suggest the undoubted truth that all through our wilderness journey we are under the eye of One who lives and sees. As the Apostle says, *"He is able also to save them to the uttermost...seeing He ever liveth to make intercession for them"* (Heb. 7:25).

THE COMING

Further we see that Isaac definitely came to meet the bride, for Rebekah inquired, *"What man is this that walketh in the field to meet us?"* The picture presents Isaac as one who was waiting for, and wanting, his bride. Our desires after Christ may often be feeble, but He longs for the moment when His bride will be presented to Him. Before He went away, He could say to His disciples, *"If I go...I will come again, and receive you unto Myself; that where I am, there ye may be also"* (Jn. 14:3).

THE MARRIAGE

When at last Rebekah saw Isaac, *"she took a veil and covered herself."* Immediately, the marriage followed, for we read, *"Isaac...took Rebekah...and she became his wife and he loved her."* So, too, after our wilderness journey, when the great work of the Holy Spirit is accomplished, and for the first time we see the Lord Jesus face to face—when He receives us to Himself—then at last these wonderful words will be fulfilled, *"The marriage of the Lamb is come, and His wife hath made herself ready."*

When creation was completed, Eve was presented to

Adam as his bride, the first type of the great mystery which from the beginning of the world has been hid in God, and which tells of God's eternal purpose to secure a bride for His Son. Through the long centuries, and amidst all changing dispensations, God has kept in view the great day of the marriage of the Lamb.

God's people may fail and break down, as they have done in every dispensation. The world, increasing in violence and corruption, may tempt and often overcome the people of God. The devil may oppose and set up the false woman who becomes drunk with the blood of saints. Nevertheless, in spite of the failure of God's people, the efforts of the devil, and the temptations of the world, God never turns aside from His great purpose to secure a bride for His Son.

At the end of God's Book, we are permitted to see in a vision the great day of the marriage of the Lamb, and at the very close we have a beautiful presentation of Jesus waiting for His bride, and the bride, in her true attitude, as led by the Spirit, looking for the coming of Jesus. *"The Spirit and the bride say, Come."* His answer is, *"Surely I come quickly,"* and the bride responds, *"Even so, come, Lord Jesus."*

The Incentive for Us

How much disappointment we would be saved if, in all our service, we had before us the great object that is always before the Spirit of God—the presentation of the Church to Christ without spot or wrinkle or any such thing on the great day of the marriage of the Lamb. Our view, and our service, is too often narrowed down to a small locality and our little day; then when everything seems to fail locally, we are brokenhearted and disappointed. If, however, our great object is to gather souls to Christ in view of the marriage of the Lamb, we shall not be disappointed, whatever the sorrow and failure by the way. There will be no broken hearts, no regrets, no disappointments when at last we hear the voice of a great multitude, as the voice of many waters, and as the voice of mighty thunderings, saying, *"Let us be glad and rejoice, and give honor to Him: for the marriage of the Lamb is come."*

Let us then press forward through sorrows, through trials, through weakness, through every kind of opposition, knowing that at the end there is the great day of the marriage of the Lamb.

The typical teaching of these chapters closes with the account of Abraham's children by Keturah, given in the first six verses of chapter 25. These children, from whom many Eastern nations have their origin, received *"gifts,"* and thus came in for blessing through their connection with Abraham. Nevertheless, Isaac was placed in striking contrast to the other sons of Abraham. To others he may have given gifts; to Isaac he gave all that he had.

This may set forth in type the great truth that Christ, as risen from the dead, is the Heir of all things, and that after receiving His heavenly bride, He will enter into the earthly inheritance in connection with restored Israel, while the nations of the earth will also receive blessing.

The deeply instructive history of Abraham closes with the brief record of his peaceful end at *"a good old age,"* and the burial by his sons Isaac and Ishmael in the cave of Machpelah. Thus in striking contrast to poor Lot, Abraham finished his pilgrim path with the respect and honor due to one who was *"the friend of God,"* and *"the father of all them that believe."*

Abraham's Memorials

Only a tomb, no more,
A future resting place
When God shall lay thee down and bid
All thy long wanderings cease.

This cave and field—no more
Canst thou thy dwelling call
That land of thine—plains, hills, woods, streams,
The stranger has it all.

Thy altar and thy tent
Are all that thou hast here.
With these content, thou passest on,
A homeless wanderer.

Thy life unrest and toil,
Thy course a pilgrimage;
Only in death thou goest up
To claim thy heritage.

A heritage of life
Beyond this guarded gloom,
A kingdom, not a field or cave,
A city, not a tomb.   —HORATIUS BONAR

APPENDIX I

how Abraham is Utilized in the New Testament

Abraham is referred to in Matthew (1:1, 2, 17; 3:9; 8:11; 22:32), Mark (12:26), Luke (1:55, 73; 3:8, 34; 13:16, 28; 16:22, 23, 24, 25, 29, 30; 19:9; 20:37), John (8:33, 37, 39, 40, 52, 53, 56, 57, 58), Acts (3:13, 25; 7:2, 8, 16, 17, 32; 13:26), Romans (4:1, 2, 3, 9, 12, 13, 16; 9:7; 11:1), 2 Corinthians (11:22); Galatians (3:6, 7, 8, 9, 14, 16, 18, 29; 4:22), Hebrews (2:16; 6:13; 7:1, 2, 4, 5, 6, 9; 11:8, 17), James (2:21, 23), and 1 Peter (3:6).

These references utilize Abraham in the following ways:

1. As the founder of the nation of Israel and the one to whom the covenant was made (Mt. 3:9; Lk. 1:55, 73; 3:8; 13:16; Jn. 8:33, 37, 39, 40; Acts 3:13, 25; 7:17; 13:26; Rom. 9:7; 11:1; 2 Cor. 11:22; Heb. 6:13)

2. As a pivotal figure in the Messianic line (Mt. 1:1, 2, 17; Lk. 3:34; Acts 7:8; Gal. 3:16; Heb. 2:16)

3. As an example of one who lives by faith, in fact, as the father of all the faithful (Mt. 8:11; Lk. 13:28; 19:9; Rom. 4:16; Gal. 3:7-9, 29; Heb. 11:8-19)

4. As a type of God the Father, perhaps the only type of the Father in the Old Testament (Jn. 8:56)

5. As a precedent for salvation by faith, apart from law (Rom. 4:1-3, 9-13; Gal. 3:6, 14, 18; Jas. 2:23)

6. As an illustration of faith being evidenced by works (Jas. 2:21)

6. As a key figure in an allegory, showing the distinctions between law and grace (Gal. 4:22-31)

7. As a confidant of God (Mt. 22:32; Mk. 12:26; Lk. 20:37; Acts 7:2, 32)

8. As associated with the blessedness of the believing dead (Lk. 16:22-25, 29-30;

9. As a highly significant historical figure (Jn. 8:52, 53, 57, 58; Acts 7:16; Heb. 7:1-2, 4)

10. As the progenitor of the Aaronic priesthood (Heb. 7:5-6, 9)

12. As a husband whose wife set an example of godly submission (1 Pet. 3:6)

APPENDIX II

Maps Showing the Journeys of Abraham

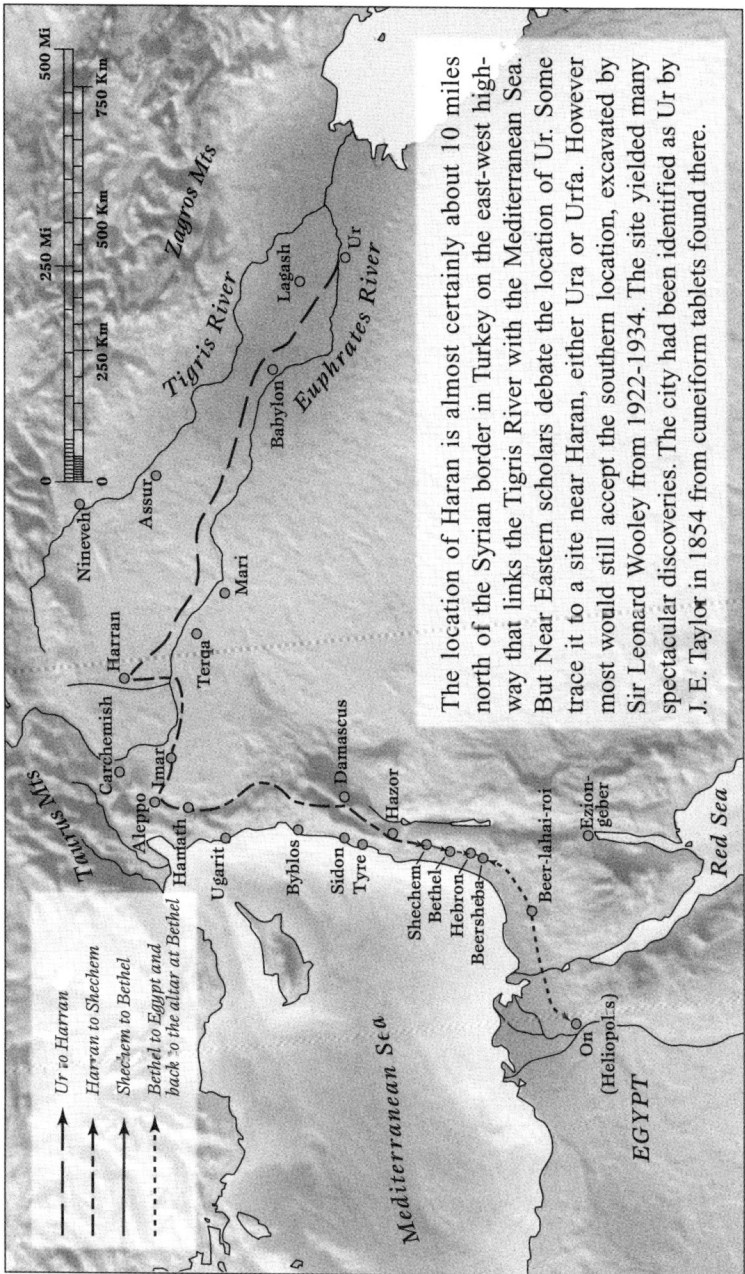

The location of Haran is almost certainly about 10 miles north of the Syrian border in Turkey on the east-west highway that links the Tigris River with the Mediterranean Sea. But Near Eastern scholars debate the location of Ur. Some trace it to a site near Haran, either Ura or Urfa. However most would still accept the southern location, excavated by Sir Leonard Wooley from 1922-1934. The site yielded many spectacular discoveries. The city had been identified as Ur by J. E. Taylor in 1854 from cuneiform tablets found there.

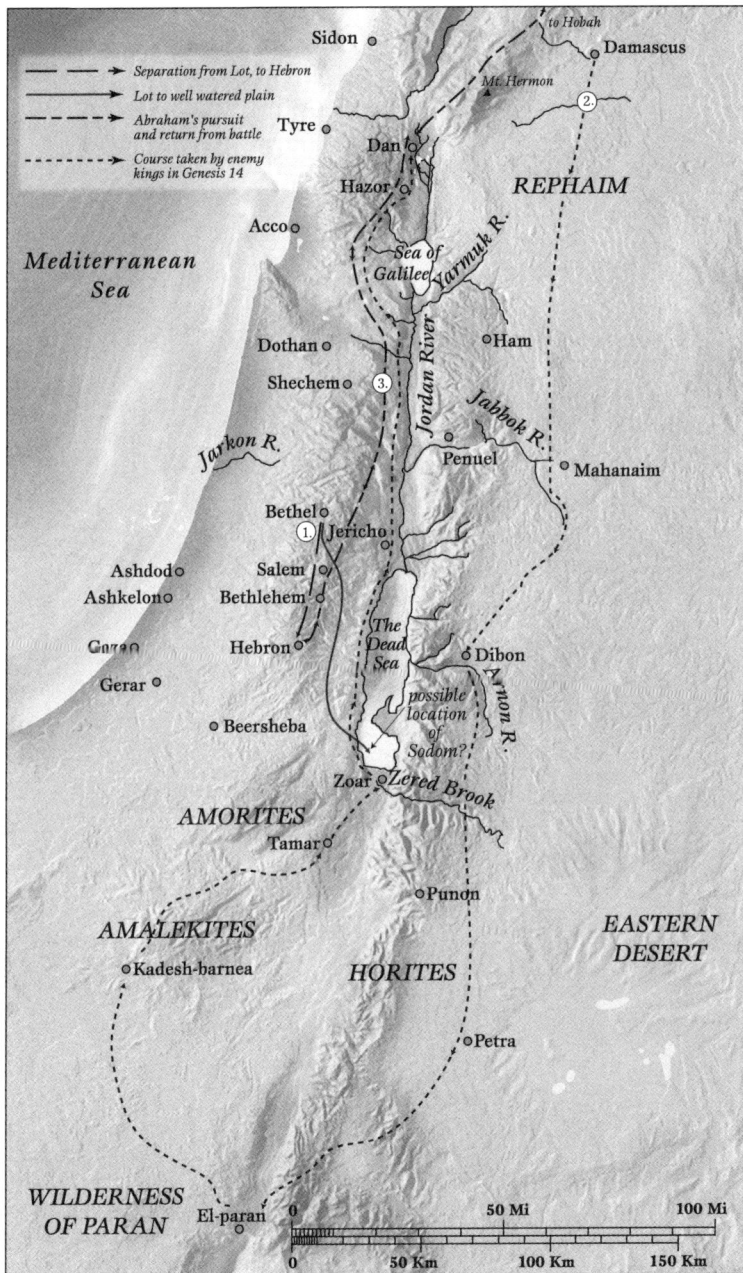

Sidon

Damascus

to Hobah

Mt. Hermon

Tyre

Dan

Hazor

REPHAIM

2

Acco

Mediterranean Sea

Sea of Galilee

Yarmuk R.

Dothan

Ham

Shechem

3.

Jordan River

Jabbok R.

Penuel

Mahanaim

Jarkon R.

Bethel

1

Jericho

Ashdod

Salem

Ashkelon

Bethlehem

Gaza

Hebron

The Dead Sea

Dibon

Arnon R.

Gerar

possible location of Sodom?

Beersheba

Zoar

Zered Brook

AMORITES

Tamar

Punon

AMALEKITES

EASTERN DESERT

Kadesh-barnea

HORITES

Petra

WILDERNESS OF PARAN

El-paran

Legend:
- — → Separation from Lot, to Hebron
- — → Lot to well watered plain
- — → Abraham's pursuit and return from battle
- ··· → Course taken by enemy kings in Genesis 14

| 0 | 50 Mi | 100 Mi |
| 0 | 50 Km | 100 Km | 150 Km |

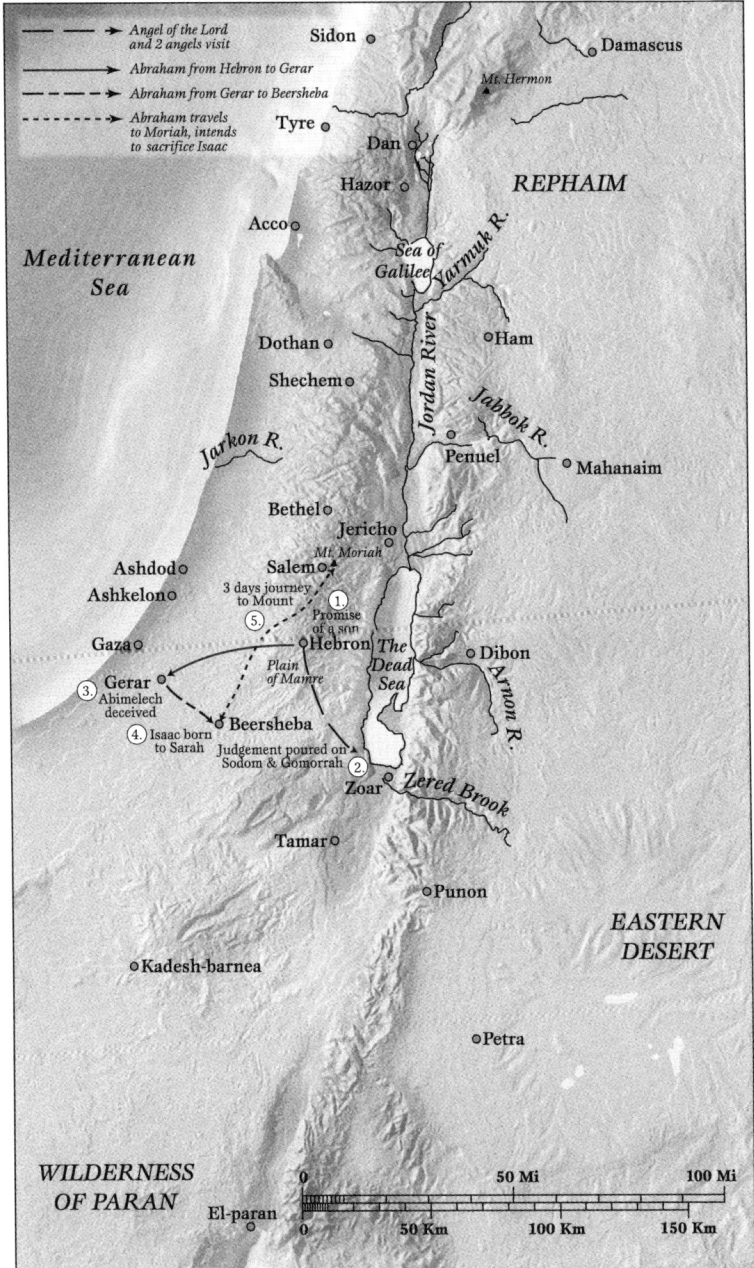

Legend:
- Angel of the Lord and 2 angels visit
- Abraham from Hebron to Gerar
- Abraham from Gerar to Beersheba
- Abraham travels to Moriah, intends to sacrifice Isaac

Sidon
Damascus
Mt. Hermon
Tyre
Dan
Hazor
REPHAIM
Acco
Mediterranean Sea
Sea of Galilee
Yarmuk R.
Jordan River
Ham
Dothan
Shechem
Jabbok R.
Jarkon R.
Penuel
Mahanaim
Bethel
Jericho
Salem
Mt. Moriah
Ashdod
Ashkelon
3 days journey to Mount
(5)
(1) Promise of a son
Gaza
Hebron
Plain of Mamre
The Dead Sea
Dibon
Arnon R.
(3) Gerar
Abimelech deceived
(4) Isaac born to Sarah
Beersheba
Judgement poured on Sodom & Gomorrah
(2)
Zoar
Zered Brook
Tamar
Punon
EASTERN DESERT
Kadesh-barnea
Petra
WILDERNESS OF PARAN
El-paran

0   50 Mi   100 Mi
0   50 Km   100 Km   150 Km

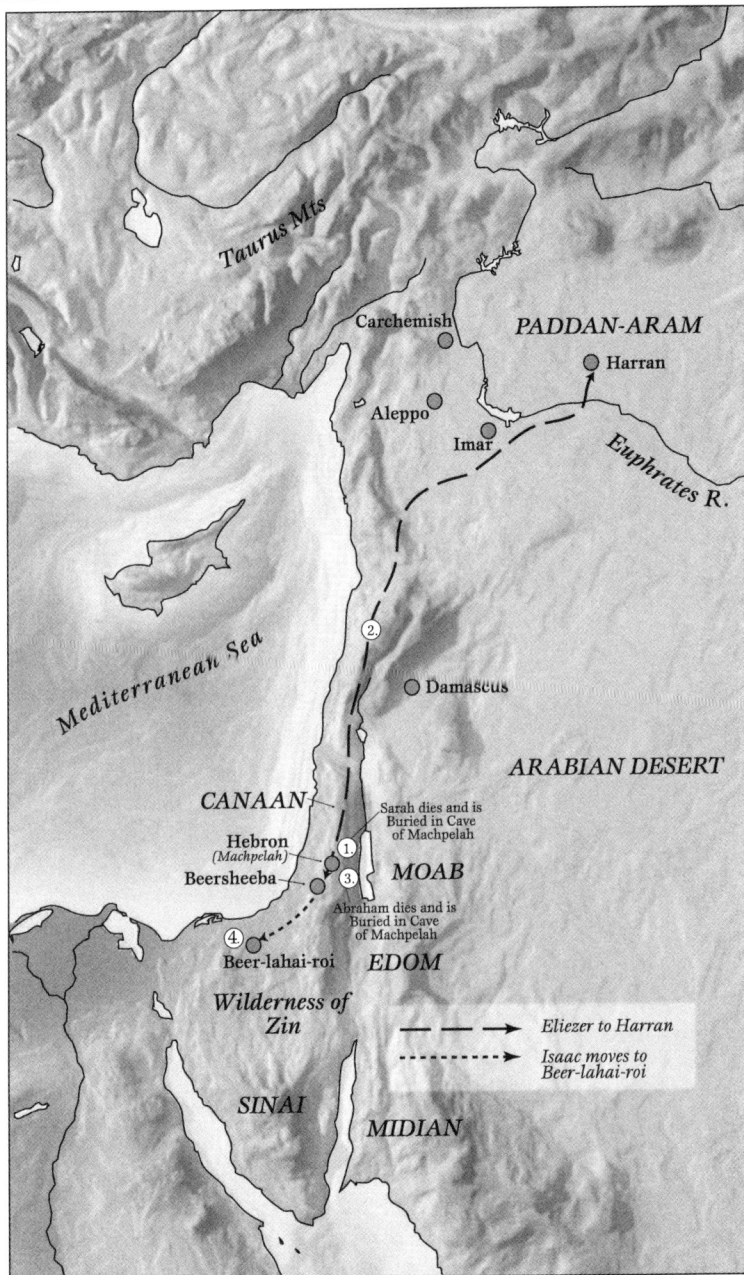

APPENDIX III

Scripture Index